GEOLOGICAL
WONDERS
of Namibia

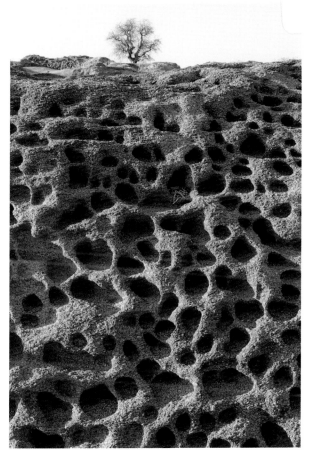

The Earth teaches us more about ourselves than

all the books in the world ...

~ Antoine de Saint-Exupéry in *Wind, Sand and Stars*, 1939 ~

GEOLOGICAL WONDERS
of Namibia

Anne-Marie & Michel Detay

Published by Struik Nature
(an imprint of Penguin Random House South Africa (Pty) Ltd)
Reg. No. 1953/000441/07
The Estuaries No. 4, Oxbow Crescent (off Century Avenue),
Century City, 7441 South Africa
PO Box 1144, Cape Town, 8000 South Africa

Visit www.penguinrandomhouse.co.za and join the Struik Nature Club
for updates, news, events and special offers.

First published in 2017

1 3 5 7 9 10 8 6 4 2

Publisher: Pippa Parker
Editor: Helen de Villiers
Design concept: Janice Evans
Designer: Dominic Robson
Cartographer: Liezel Bohdanowicz
Proofreader and indexer: Thea Grobbelaar

Reproduction by Hirt & Carter Cape (Pty) Ltd
Printed and bound by C & C Offset Printing Co., Ltd, China

Print: 9781775842941
ePub: 9781775842958
ePDF: 9781775842965

Penguin Random House is committed to a sustainable future
for our business, our readers and our planet. This book is
made from Forest Stewardship Council ® certified paper.

Front cover: Lichen growing on basalt volcanic rock
Back cover: Highly eroded boulders resulting from a dyke injection across the sands of the Namib Desert
Half-title page: Honeycomb-structured granite
Title page: Large dolerite injections cutting through granite and gneiss metamorphic complex

www.detayphoto.com

CONTENTS

ACKNOWLEDGEMENTS

Our sincere thanks and deepest appreciation to: Pippa Parker, Publisher at Struik Nature and Struik Travel, for enthusiastically believing in our geology and photography project and starting up with us an exciting publishing adventure. Helen de Villiers, Managing Editor, for the understanding of our common goal, for the enthusiasm and unending patience after long days and months spent on sometimes difficult texts, and for respecting last-minute wishes or changes always with a smile. Designers Janice Evans and Dominic Robson for crafting a wonderful book where photography and texts resonate in a beautiful and effective manner. And to the four of them for making it all work between Hong Kong, France and South Africa.

Pascaline Zicavo who started dreaming about the wonders of the Skeleton Coast as a child in the 60s and deeply influenced the dreams of the wilderness of her elder sister, Anne-Marie.

Lily and Marcel Jouve, old friends and authors of *Secret Namibia* who convinced us to come, discover and marvel at the nature of Namibia.

Good old friends who travelled all the way to Namibia with us to share precious moments of our wild adventures: young film director Sylvain Cruiziat, Patrick and Martine Sanchez, Yves Lachèvre.

Uwe and Janet Trümper who provided much-needed assistance and a friendly welcome at their home over the years.

Lewis and Ramon Druker, Thozama, and Gabbs at Coastways Tours, Lüderitz, for their exclusive 4x4 tours in the Namib Desert (Saddle Hill and Lüderitz-Walvis Bay).

Gérald Favre from the NAMGROWS (NAMibian GROundWater Systems) expedition for providing some photos of his exploration into the Dragon's Breath cave. Toni Hanke and Albert Hess at the High Energy Stereoscopic System (HESS) Cherenkov telescope, for taking us into black holes, quasars, active galactic nuclei (AGN), dark accelerators, gamma ray bursts, microquasars, superbubbles, dwarf spheroidal galaxies …

Dr Laurie Marker from the Cheetah Conservation Fund (CCF), Anne Schmidt-Küntzel, Patricia and Ryan, who all gave us lots of their precious time and provided so many explanations about the iconic cat of Namibia: the cheetah.

Beauty, the friendliest and most unforgettable black-and-white cat in the whole of southern Africa, for welcoming us at each of our stays at Melani van den Berg's Kleines Nest B&B in Walvis Bay.

The welcoming and caring staff of so many hotels, lodges and campsites where we have stayed and felt at home during our Namibian adventures: Oyster Box in Walvis Bay; Okonjima from the Africat Foundation; Otjitotongwe Cheetah Guest Farm; Kücki from Rostock Ritz Desert Lodge; Bush Pillow Guest House in Otjiwarongo; Sarel Lacante and Leoni Pretorius, owners of the Dragon Breath and Harasib caves; Mika at the Ghaub Cave; the superb staff of Wilderness Safari; superwoman Angela Carstens in Bagatelle; Manus and Lara Kotze and their private Kalahari sand dune; Douw Steyn, the Kalahari Lion whisperer at Kalahari Game Lodge, together with Sam and Nicky; Willem and Hannetjie van Rooyen at Barchan Dune Retreat; Thomas Miller and his personal rock-art discovery at the family-owned Aubure campsite; Giel Steenkamp at Mesosaurus Camp, and friendly Finn, Eleini Radeck at Kameldorn Garten in Otjiwarongo.

And many beautiful encounters on the way: world travellers Roberta Scarano and Roberto Papi during the most amazing lion encounter of our lives; Ina and Peter de Vries and their 'dune-flying' car; Shannon McEwan and his children Brogan and Ambrin; Franca and Adrian Schmidlin with their children Simon, Anya and Fabian; Teresa Valdes-Sanchez, our Cheetah-Lady Spanish friend; Dorothee Wiktorin and Detlef Kleinert, together with the Kalahari Lions Noop and Nick; Agnès, Marion, Emma and Rose, the super girls of the Michel family; Ulrich and Catherine Müller with Oshiwa the leopard at Africat; Nico Burger and his incredible V8 Toyota; Felix and Colette, and Victor and Claire-Françoise Stresemann with their four world-hungry children.

And, of course, the best friends of our globetrotter and all-terrain-proof Toyota Land Cruiser: Ian and Petrus from Toyota Otjiwarongo; Dirk Bosman, owner of Namib off-road Centre in Walvis Bay; Arno at the Toyota garage in Walvis Bay; and Gert Jacobs from Mariental Toyota.

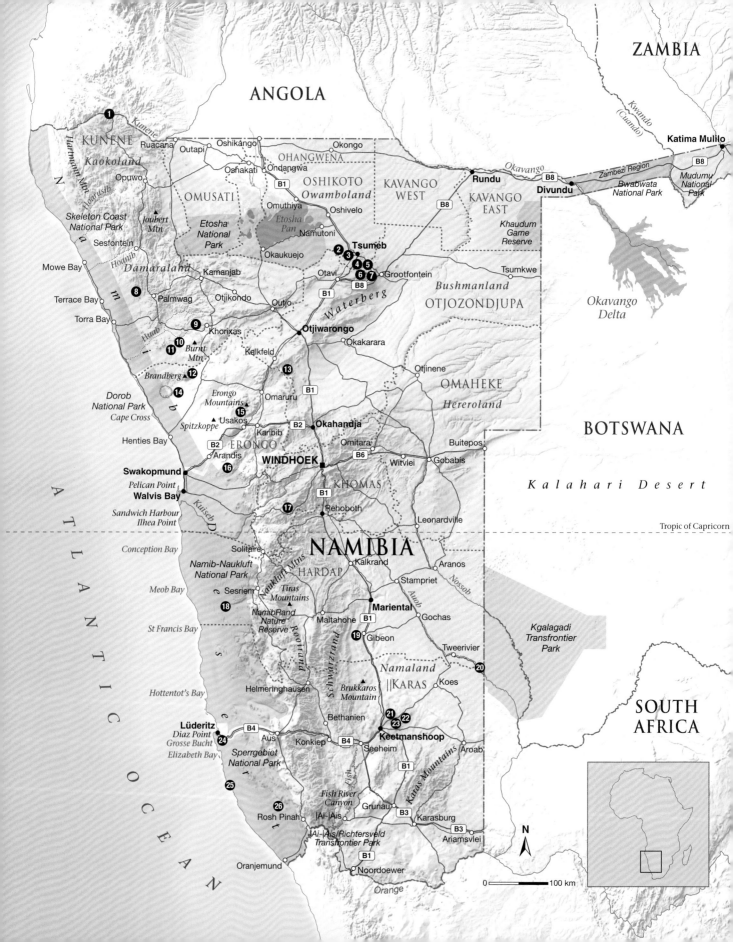

SOME FEATURES OF THE NAMIBIAN LANDSCAPE

1. Epupa Falls
2. Lake Guinas
3. Otjikoto Lake
4. Ghaub Cave
5. Dragon's Breath Cave
6. Harasib Cave
7. Hoba meteorite
8. Etendeka Large Igneous Province
9. Khorixas Petrified Forest
10. Twyfelfontein
11. Valley of the Organ Pipes
12. White Lady
13. Otjihaenamaparero
14. Messum Crater
15. Ameib Ranch
16. Wustenquell
17. H.E.S.S. site
18. Sossusvlei
19. Gibeon Kimberlite-Carbonatite Province
20. Kalahari Game Lodge
21. Gariganus Farm
22. Giant's Playground
23. Mesosaurus Fossil Bush Camp
24. Kolmanskop
25. Klein Bogenfels
26. Roter Kamm Crater

TERMS AND ABBREVIATIONS USED

Billions of years (ago) = **Ga**
Millions of years (ago) = **Ma**
Kilometre = **km**
Metre = **m**
Hectare = **ha**

MILESTONES OF NAMIBIAN GEOLOGY

The surface of the Earth once looked completely different: vast oceans covered most of the planet, dotted with islands of early landmasses, called 'cratons'. Over millions of years, through craton amalgamation, opening and closing of palaeo-oceans, rifting, subduction and mountain-building events, the land as we know it was built in a process called 'global tectonics'. Mountain ranges formed, only to be followed by massive erosion, when thousands of metres of terrain were washed down to the oceans or deposited on lowlands and in valleys – processes driven by extreme weather conditions and climatic variations. Namibia was at the heart of the action, also experiencing extensive glaciation and 'snowball Earth' events, followed by widespread deglaciation.

Between Keetmanshoop and Lüderitz, the sands – stained red by iron-rich minerals – are anchored by wind-blasted vegetation, with occasional termite mounds punctuating the open vista.

The Earth has a long history, starting some 4.5 billion years ago (4.5 Ga), when it formed from the accretion of objects orbiting the sun (**Chapter 1**), as well as from meteorites originating outside our solar system (**Chapter 2**). The geological history of Namibia itself is very old and complex as it encompasses some 2.65 Ga of Earth's history.

Ongoing plate tectonic movement was accompanied by cataclysmic volcanic and plutonic activity. The oldest rocks found in Namibia (**Chapter 3**) were formed 2.65 Ga in the Middle Precambrian. They make up what are known as 'metamorphic complexes', meaning they have undergone several cycles of metamorphism (where structural change happens as a result of heat, pressure or other natural agency) during waves of mountain building, or orogeny – the first two being the Vaalian (2.1–1.759 Ga) and Mokolian (1.759–0.9 Ga). The nature of the original rocks, before being affected by metamorphism, is often unknown; but they are remants of the Congo Craton (in the north) and Kalahari Craton (in the south) that merged to form first the Rodinia supercontinent (1.3–0.9 Ga) and, more recently, the Gondwana supercontinent (900–600 million years ago, or Ma) – cratons being the large stable blocks of crust that underpin the continents. These ancient rocks can be found in the Hoarusib Valley and in the Kunene Region. In southern Namibia, the ground we walk on is composed of rocks from the Namaqua Metamorphic Complex, deposited more than 1.8 Ga, and visible at the bottom of the Fish River Canyon (**Chapter 4**).

The presence of groundwater, which fills the porous spaces between grains of sand and in rocks, enables some mammal species to survive in arid surroundings, including these hardy African elephants in northern Namibia.

A third wave of mountain building, known as the Damara Orogen, took place when the Congo and Kalahari cratons collided. The area between the two cratons had been a shallow sea, the Khomas Ocean, and the collision of the cratons resulted in the formation of Alpine or Andes-type mountain belts called the Damara Mountain range. Central Namibia was an active volcanic zone, and intrusions accompanied the mountain-building process between 650 and 460 Ma. More than 200 extensively mineralized granitic plutons intruded the Damara Sequence during this period.

The Otavi region in northern Namibia is composed of some 5,000 km² of limestone terrains and numerous stromatolites. Karstic weathering in this region led to the development of caves, cenotes (**Chapter 5**) and huge underground lakes.

As the tectonic plates drifted across the Earth's surface, Namibia came to be located at the South Pole, and was covered by a huge ice sheet, before plate tectonic movements linked to the subsequent opening of the South Atlantic Ocean nudged southern Africa northwards. This heralded a period of more moderate climatic conditions: melting of the ice sheet provided ample water to create an environment with huge lakes and rivers, in which grey to green-weathering shales, mudstones, limestones, sandstones and coal-bearing shales were deposited. Large trees, swept downstream in the flood conditions, and covered by alluvial sand, are now preserved as the petrified wood of Khorixas.

Smaller sedimentary basins developed in Namibia too, in which the *Mesosaurus* would have thrived; records of this land reptile that had returned to an aquatic habitat are now preserved as the Mesosaurus fossils (**Chapter 6**). During the Late Paleozoic, the Mesosaurus inland sea covered vast areas (~5 million km^2) of the southwest interior of Gondwana, extending from the southern margins of South Africa to northern Namibia and westwards into Brazil and Uruguay. The correlation between fossils in the Paraná Basin in South America and those in southern Africa was key evidence in support of the plate tectonic theory.

The Damara Supergroup (850–535 Ma) deposition, resulting largely from the erosion of the Damara Mountain range, includes two of the best-known examples of the 'snowball Earth' glaciations (**Chapter 7**). Extensive, ongoing erosion of the Damaran Mountain belt was the source of the Karoo Sequence deposition, some 300–135 Ma. By the end of the Carboniferous, 200 million years of erosion had left only remnants of the Damara Mountain belt, resulting in vast peneplains that are evident today. Rocks of the Permo-Carboniferous to Jurassic Karoo Sequence were later to be deposited on these plains.

During the Cretaceous and Tertiary, southern Africa completed its separation from the neighbouring parts of Gondwanaland, and extensive volcanism (**Chapter 8**) – an expression of tension as a result of plate tectonic movements – resulted in the lavas of the Etendeka Plateau, as well as numerous dolerite intrusions, such as Namibia's dyke swarms, or Giant's Playground near Keetmanshoop. During the Early Cretaceous some 133–132 Ma, a major wind-driven system – a sand sea – was active across much of southern Gondwana. Sediments deposited during this period are preserved in the Huab Basin.

Complex, layered intrusions (**Chapters 9, 10 and 11**), such as the Brandberg, aged 137–130 Ma, occur in a zone extending from the coast north of Swakopmund in a northeasterly direction. They are not related to mountain building, but are thought to result from hot mantle plume activity – the St Helena–Gough–Walvis volcanic chain.

Plate tectonic activity led to the opening of the South Atlantic Ocean, and to volcanic eruptions and continental uplift; and so the sedimentary Kalahari Basin was formed in the centre of the subcontinent, surrounded by a great escarpment. Meanwhile, severe changes of environmental conditions during the Jurassic led to the establishment of an extremely arid climate. In the Cenozoic, the Kalahari Desert (**Chapter 12**) developed in northern and eastern Namibia, and calcrete formed in the Etosha region.

More recently, humans evolved in southern Africa. They left much rock art, such as the White Lady in the Brandberg or carvings in Twyfelfontein on the Etjo sandstones deposited 180 million years ago. These in turn became both an arena, and the tools used by humans, for rock art (**Chapter 13**). This is what geology and geomorphology are about: a mix of huge processes of plate tectonic activity, weathering and redeposition, leading to the creation of amazing landforms and landscapes, gems and minerals (**Chapter 14**).

Today, about half of the Namibian surface consists of bedrock; the other half is covered by desert sands forming the Kalahari and Namib deserts. Geological mechanisms are still at work today in this land of deserts and pans, groundwater and aquifers (**Chapter 15**); tectonic activity and weathering are still creating improbable landscapes: the south Atlantic hot spot plume system and the East African rift system are active; desertification and climatic changes are happening. The geological wonders of Namibia are still very much in progress.

Following pages

This desolate moonscape near Swakopmund gradually formed through erosion of the Swakop River in the Damara granites (dated 500–460 Ma).

Impermanence rules: once part of the infrastructure of frenetic diamond mining, this railway station now rests, empty and silent, right in the middle of the desert.

CHAPTER 1

HOW IT ALL BEGAN

Most visitors to Namibia come to wonder at the beauty of unspoiled nature and to view the wildlife. But some come all the way to this remote southern African land specifically for stargazing. Thanks to the relative absence of both industrial and urban light pollution in the Namib Desert, the nights are considered to be among the darkest on the planet, and offer largely unobstructed views of the night sky. Consequently, this ancient desert was recently named an 'international dark sky reserve', one of only 10 in the world.

In some areas of the country, not only do stars fill the sky – they seem to be growing on trees too. This is the quiver tree *(Aloe dichotoma)*, or kokerboom, from the hollow branches of which San hunters used to make quivers for their arrows. These trees are endemic to the Northern Cape region of South Africa and to southern Namibia.

13.8 BILLION YEARS AGO

LOOKING INTO EARTH'S STRUCTURE

The universe was formed by the Big Bang approximately 13.8 billon years ago (Ga), and our particular solar system was formed 4.567 Ga from elements present within the protosolar cloud. Everything material on our planet – rocks, trees, water, smartphones, paper, marble statues, sand dunes, diamonds, and humans too – is made of atoms. And every one of these billions upon billions of atoms has been formed through stellar processes: through the birth, life and death of stars within the universe.

Looking up at the night sky and trying to understand its secrets is to reach out to the very substance that forms our planet and everything in and on it.

TRAVELLING BACK IN TIME

Scanning the night sky is a form of time travel. For instance, Sirius, a star that can easily be spotted by the human eye, is located 8 light years away from our planet. So when we look up at Sirius, the light we see is actually 8 years old.

Using visual aids, we can travel much further back in time. With binoculars, we can easily spot Andromeda, which is 2 million light years away; and with a simple telescope we can travel even further, all the way back to 50 million light years away. Professional telescopes can take us back billions of light years – to the start of the universe itself.

This mind-boggling journey back in time is what has enabled astronomers to understand and explain the formation of the planet we call home, of our own solar system and of the universe itself.

FEELING PART OF THE UNIVERSE

Namibia offers one of the best spots on Earth for experiencing our connection to the universe. This requires no more than simply standing outdoors on a moonless night, head up, eyes wide open. The Milky Way appears in full splendour and with astounding clarity, showing billions of stars and masses of gas and dust. It feels as if you can almost reach up and touch this arc of light, which is our home galaxy – one of just many billions of other galaxies in the universe.

Opposite

On this ancient rocky Namibian surface, which 250 Ma ago was part of the primitive Gondwana supercontinent, one may get little sleep at night: the sky calls adventurers to travel the Milky Way, in silence and perhaps in the company of imaginary companions, also made of stardust.

Following pages

Branches of leafless botterboom (Tylecodon paniculatus), indigenous to Namibia, seem to stretch their arms and fingers to reach out into the crystal-clear Namibian night, filled with magnificent concentrations of stars, cosmic gases and dusts.

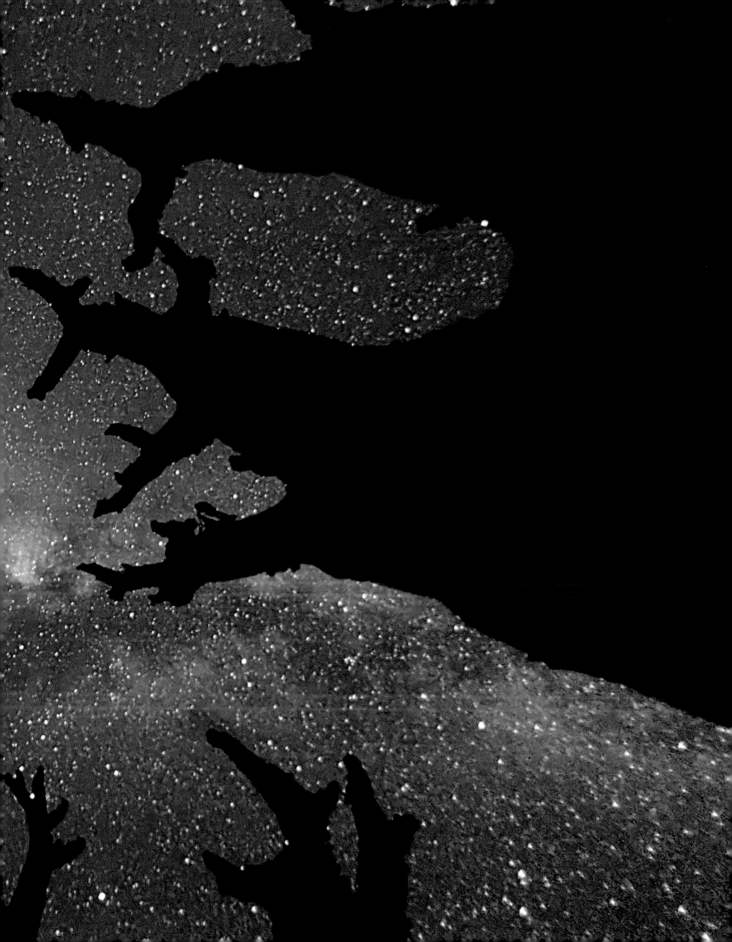

WITNESSING OUTER SPACE TRAFFIC

The crisp night sky of Namibia brings further rewards: huge numbers of 'shooting stars'. These mostly tiny particles, often no more than the size of a grain of sand, are travellers from outer space that have entered Earth's atmosphere, where they rapidly burn up.

Larger bodies, called 'Near-Earth Objects' (NEOs), cruise through outer space too and sometimes enter our atmosphere as meteors. Such extraterrestrial bodies occasionally survive their trip through the atmosphere and land on Earth. Depending on their size, meteorites (as landed bodies are called) can have catastrophic effects. Some are thought to have triggered mass extinctions during the last 500 million years. A very large impact 65 Ma is linked to the demise of the dinosaurs – creating space for the emergence of other life forms, in this case, the mammals.

ACCESSING THE MOST POWERFUL ENERGY (HESS)

Because of its crisp, clear skies and because its latitude is well suited to observations of the Galactic Centre, the area near the Gamsberg Mountains is home to the world's largest gamma-ray observatory, the High Energy Stereoscopic System (HESS).

This observatory has been ranked the tenth most influential observatory in the world, competing with others as famous as the Hubble Space Telescope. Inaugurated in 2004 with four telescopes, and extended in 2012 with the addition of a much larger telescope, the HESS operates as a stereoscopic viewing system of atmospheric gamma-ray showers through its five telescopes of varying sizes.

Gamma rays – the most energetic rays in the universe – are our best way of observing cosmic particle accelerators such as supernova remnants and pulsar wind nebulae, all end products of massive imploding stars. Because of Namibia's position on the planet, the HESS has access to, and can observe the central regions of our galaxy where a great number of cosmic objects are located, such as supernovae, pulsars, active galactic nuclei, dark accelerators, gamma-ray bursts, micro-quasars and black holes.

Visiting HESS is incomparably better than watching *Star Wars*!

HESS is a stereoscopic telescope system where multiple telescopes simultaneously view and capture air showers of particles, generated by high-energy gamma rays interacting high up in the atmosphere. This impressively huge single dish named the 'HESS II Telescope' is 32.6 m x 24.3 m (equivalent to a 28 m-diameter circular dish), weighs 580 tonnes and displays a total mirror area of 614 m². The telescope enables unparalleled observation of high-energy processes in the universe. The observatory is operated by a collaboration of more than 260 scientists from some 40 scientific institutions and 13 different countries. Photographing this otherwordly vessel and seeing oneself reflected in one of the mirrors – centre bottom of the picture – is an unsettling experience.

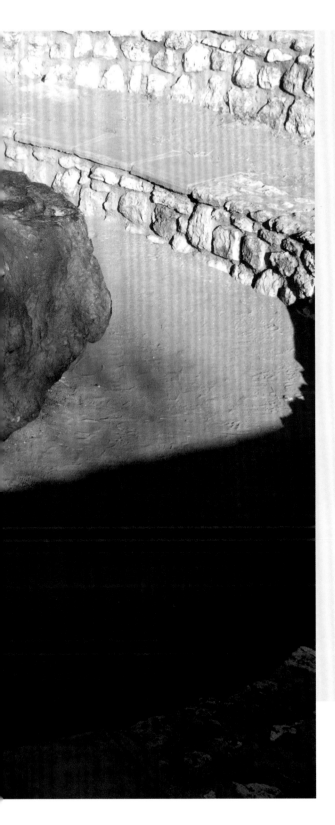

CHAPTER 2

METEORITES

Namibia offers visitors just about the best opportunities on Earth for visiting meteorite landing sites, as well as the chance of seeing and touching the celestial objects themselves. What makes meteorites particularly exciting is the knowledge that they are samples of the very building blocks of which our solar system is composed, and that lie at the core of our own planet.

The Hoba meteorite remains where it was originally found – near Grootfontein in northern Namibia. The largest known such body on Earth, it is believed to have landed 80,000 years ago. It was declared a Namibian national monument on 15 March 1955. An amphitheatre-type surround now helps protect it against vandalism.

4.567 BILLION YEARS AGO

SHOOTING STARS

Meteors, or 'shooting stars' as they are often called, are small rocks or dust particles in space that enter Earth's atmosphere and are often seen streaking dramatically through the night sky. Most burn up before making landfall, but those that do reach the ground are known as 'meteorites'. To date, they are our only samples of material coming from beyond the Earth-Moon system. Most of the approximately 40,000 tonnes of extraterrestrial material that reach Earth each year arrive unnoticed, as mere dust particles. Some solid bodies do land, however, even though scarred and depleted from the course of their fiery journey.

Meteors travel through Earth's atmosphere at a speed of between 39,600 km/h and 108,000 km/h, depending on whether they travel with or against the Earth's cruising direction around the Sun. Friction with the atmosphere turns the speeding bodies into bright fireballs as their surface melts and boils and is sometimes ripped off in a process known as 'ablation'. So hot do the fragments become that remarkable, characteristic pull-out surface features form, resembling impressions in clay, and called 'regmaglypts'. When meteors land, their surface solidifies, usually forming a dark grey to black fusion crust. Some have pointed to fusion crusts as the inspiration for the contemporary metal sculptures of Henry Moore and Alberto Giacometti.

Most meteors fragment as they pass through successive layers of the Earth's atmosphere, sometimes creating a meteor shower. Those larger than about 100 tonnes and solid enough to resist fragmentation strike the ground at hypersonic velocity, exploding on impact. Often the entire body is destroyed in the process – as at the Roter Kamm site in southern Namibia; but sometimes fragments survive, and can be found within or around the impact crater.

WITNESSES TO OUR ORIGINS

Regarded as the 'Rosetta Stones' of astronomical research, meteorites are key to our understanding of the origin and early history of our solar system, which formed some 4,567 Ga. It is thought that our solar nebula formed when a star cataclysmically blew up, scattering the resulting dust and gas outwards into space. The scattered material gradually agglomerated into millimetre-sized spherules of silicate, known as 'chondrules', the building blocks of stony meteorites. These spherules, in turn, agglomerated into bigger bodies, forming protoplanets of 10–100 km in diameter. As the protoplanets grew, they attracted heavy materials, like iron and nickel, towards their centre, in a process known as 'differentiation'.

Gradually, our solar system's planets formed into the bodies we know today. With the gradual decrease in the number of individual bodies – and so in the number of impacts – the early chaos of the solar system quietened down. But meteors still cruise endlessly through space, and some are destined to be trapped by the gravitational pull of the planets.

PAST AND PRESENT IMPACTS

Celestial impacts and volcanism are recognized as the two main geological processes at work in the solar system. Comets and meteors are constantly on the move and risk intersecting with the paths of planets; impacts in the past have left their mark in the form of craters, some of which are still visible today.

The demise of the dinosaurs has been linked to a catastrophic impact that formed Mexico's huge, now buried, Chicxulub impact structure some 65 Ma, although the massive eruption of flood basalts, such as the Paraná-Etendeka traps in northwest Namibia/southwest Angola, has also been considered a possible cause.

Namibia's Roter Kamm meteorite impact crater (-27.767093°/16.290464°) is a strikingly well-preserved feature. With a diameter of 2.5 km, it has a rim that rises 140 m above the surrounding desert plain and 160 m above the crater floor. Rare pieces of impact 'melt glass' associated with the crater, and resulting from the energy released during impact, when rock and soil are melted and then harden to form 'glass', have an age of 3.7 Ma.

Another huge impact structure has been identified in Namibia: the Karas impact structure, which has been dated as being pre-Nama in age, or more than 1,350 Ga.

The Roter Kamm meteorite impact crater forms a distinct and clearly recognizable circular feature that is, unfortunately, visible only from above. Direct access is forbidden as the crater (located 60 km east of the coast, 70 km from the South African border and 50 km west of the mining town of Rosh Pinah) falls within the 'Sperrgebiet', or Prohibited Zone.

© Christian Koeberl – University of Vienna, Austria

The journey of the Hoba meteorite through Earth's atmosphere has left marks, known as 'ablation scars', on the iron surface of this celestial body. These visible scars are the signature of melted material that has left the meteorite during its flight through our planetary atmosphere, and flown into the airstream behind the fireball. Ablation is responsible for a significant loss of mass in meteorites.

The collision of comet Shoemaker-Levy 9 with Jupiter in July 1994 released energy estimated to have been 600 times the world's current nuclear arsenal, and would probably have been enough to wipe out life on Earth.

NASA is involved in NEO (Near-Earth Objects) research with a view to preventing such a catastrophe, although the likelihood of a collision is remote. Only two relatively minor events have been recorded (both in Asia) over the last century: the 1908 Tunguska event in Siberia, in which a comet or meteorite exploded just above a forest, flattening some 80 million trees; and the 2013 Chelyabinsk meteorite, which wounded 1,500 people and damaged some 7,000 buildings.

DIFFERENT TYPES OF METEORITES

Meteorites are assigned to one of three different categories, based on their composition: iron meteorites (about 4% of all falls) consist almost entirely of iron-nickel and are thought to belong to the iron core of a fragmenting protoplanet that cooled and crystallized over thousands of years; stony meteorites consist of silicates (a group of rock-forming minerals); and stony-iron meteorites consist of roughly equal proportions of metals and silicates.

At least 18 meteorites – or fragments of meteorites – have been found in Namibia.

NAMIBIA'S FAMOUS METEORITES

The **Hoba meteorite** in Namibia is the largest known meteorite on Earth; no other fragments of this body have been found in the surrounding area, suggesting it travelled through Earth's atmosphere without ever fragmenting. Weighing about 60 tonnes, this iron meteorite was found near Grootfontein and is thought to have landed some 80,000 years ago. It is composed mostly of iron (82,4%) and nickel (16,4%), with some cobalt and various trace elements such as carbon, sulphur, chromium, copper, zinc, gallium, germanium and iridium. Iron meteorites come from the disintegrating cores of asteroids, a belt of bodies in orbit between Mars and Jupiter.

This meteorite was found in 1920 by Jacobus Hermanus Brits while he was ploughing his land, just over 19 km west of Grootfontein. The document in which he described his find can still be seen at the Grootfontein Museum. It was initially thought that this bounty of nickel could profitably be mined; but recovering nickel from a 60-tonne chunk of solid metal soon proved unrealistic and was abandoned. In 1954, the curator of the American Museum of Natural History in New York City attempted to purchase the Hoba for display at the NYC museum. Luckily, the railway line's incapacity to transport such a huge load meant the meteorite could not be moved, and it can still be seen at its original impact point: -19.592522°/17.933685°.

During prehistoric times, another meteor, measuring roughly 4 x 4 x 1.5 m, entered the Earth's atmosphere at a low angle of 10–20° from the horizon. As it penetrated the atmosphere, the meteor went through extremely violent fragmentation, shattering into multiple pieces and creating a meteorite shower that might have been witnessed from the ground as a fireball streaking through the sky. These fragments fell over a vast strewn field, an elliptical area of 360 km long and 135 km wide (27,500 km²) southeast of the small village of Gibeon in central Namibia. The **Gibeon meteorite**, also iron, has an estimated total mass that places it among some of the biggest known such bodies on Earth. Geochemical dating gives the age of solidification of the parent body to the Gibeon meteorite as 4 Ga. To date, some 120 specimens of the Gibeon have been recorded, ranging from a few grams up to a tonne, with a collective mass of approximately 26 tonnes. Fragments were first discovered by the Nama people, and were used by them to make tools and weapons. Over the last few decades, several

Left

Meteorites provide material that enables us to explore outer space. This scar on the surface of the Hoba meteorite was made by humans for the purpose of sampling and analysis.

Opposite

Extraordinary 'Widmanstatten' patterns emerge after acid-etching a polished surface of iron meteorites – in this case, of a Gibeon meteorite fragment. These patterned fragments are valuable components in jewellery. Advertisements can justifiably make claims such as 'Dare to use a stone that is truly out of this world'.

tonnes of Gibeon meteorite fragments have been found. This extensive harvesting means it is difficult to find any new specimens without a dedicated metal detector.

A stony meteorite, **Korra Korrabes**, was also recovered in Namibia from a site just south of the town of Mariental.

COLLECTABLE GEMS

It is strictly forbidden to collect meteorites in Namibia or to have them shipped abroad. However, an unrecorded number of Gibeon meteorite fragments have been collected and have left the country illegally to be sold at international shows and auctions.

The community of meteorite enthusiasts and collectors has burgeoned worldwide, and includes the rich and famous, who all help push up prices at auctions for a chance to own a piece of cosmic material. What fuels such an expensive hobby? Firstly, meteorites are rare: the complete mass of landed meteorites per year is less than the world's daily output of gold. And secondly, they carry the magic of outer space with them: they represent a minuscule piece of extraterrestrial real estate. Good enough reasons to explain why, in the last few decades, this scarce material has become one of the most desirable collectables.

The Gibeon meteorite is probably the most sought-after meteorite among knowledgeable collectors. Because of its exceptional Widmanstatten patterns and rust-proof qualities, it is even used in jewellery, in particular by world-famous American jeweller David Yurman, who has created a 'meteorite collection' using the stones.

CHAPTER 3

THE OLDEST ROCKS IN NAMIBIA

Geological dating has been revolutionized over the last century, thanks to new discoveries and advances in radiometry. However, using these new methods requires a sophisticated approach and thorough, holistic understanding of the geological history of a region before a meaningful age can be attributed to the local rocks. Without this knowledge, gross errors can be made, as the measured age of rocks always relates only to the most recent metamorphic and/or fluid circulation event they have undergone. These events reset the geological clock whenever they occur, and so mask the rocks' original age of formation, potentially leading to wrong conclusions. A geologist needs to analyse age data with a detective's curiosity.

Seen here at the border of the Sperregebiet of the Namib Desert, the Huab Metamorphic Complex, thought to be 1.9–1.7 Ga, is one of the very few remnants of the Congo Craton. As it has undergone many formation and deformation events, the characteristics of the original rock formation have been partially erased – the reason it is referred to as a 'metamorphic complex'.

2.645 BILLION YEARS AGO

THE RADIOMETRIC CLOCK

The discovery in the 1950s that radioactivity can be used to date rocks triggered a revolution in the field of geology as it suddenly enabled the accurate dating of our planet's building blocks. Since then, radiometry has been a powerful and largely reliable method that has enabled geoscientists not only to ascertain the ages of physical entities such as the Earth, the Moon, Mars, meteorites and mineral deposits, but also to extrapolate the dates of many geological events and processes, such as the emergence of early humans, periodic glaciations and the recurrence rates of volcanic eruptions.

Elements that emit radiation have been part of the Earth ever since the solar system formed 4.56 Ga. Consequently, every rock and mineral on our planet contains, to some degree, radioactive elements. These elements are unstable, naturally breaking down over time into more stable atoms in a process known as 'radioactive decay'.

The old Tiras Mountains in southwestern Namibia still stand tall at the edge of the Namib Desert as witnesses of the region's geological origins. Now significantly eroded, these are mere remnants of the Mesoproterozoic mountain-building events that took place some 1,600–1,000 Ma.

Atoms of the radioactive elements have different forms, called 'isotopes'. Each original isotope, called the 'parent', gradually decays over time to form a new isotope, called the 'daughter'. For example, when a 'parent' isotope uranium-238 decays, it produces subatomic particles, energy, and a 'daughter' isotope lead-206. Radiometric clocks are 'set' when each rock forms – at the moment when an igneous rock solidifies from liquid magma, or a sedimentary rock layer is deposited, or a rock that has been heated by metamorphism cools off. Radioactive decay occurs at a constant rate that is specific to each radioactive isotope. These rates of decay are known, so by measuring the proportion of parent-to-daughter isotopes in rocks, it's possible to calculate when the rocks were formed.

Because of their unique decay rates, different elements found within the rocks are suitable for dating different age ranges: for instance, decay of potassium-40 to argon-40 is used to date rocks older than 20,000 years, while decay of uranium-238 to lead-206 is used for rocks older than 1 million years and up to the age of the Earth.

While this radiometric dating technique has revolutionized our understanding of geology, the results are only credible when teamed with a comprehensive study of the regional environment and its history.

At the very heart of the Epupa Metamorphic Complex, the Kunene River, which marks the boundary between Namibia and Angola, plunges down the fault in roaring cascades, sending up a cloud of mist.

EPUPA METAMORPHIC COMPLEX

The strikingly beautiful Epupa Falls on the northern border with Angola (where they are known as the Monte Negro Falls) form Namibia's crown. The falls make for magical scenery: a series of many waterfalls plunging down a razor-slit geological fault; lush vegetation; small islands covered with moss; staggering Makalani palms everywhere; and an army of watchful baobabs standing defiantly above the raging chasm – sights and scenes that are entirely unexpected in this mostly arid, flat and barren land.

The Epupa Metamorphic Complex (EMC) is one of the oldest rock formations in Namibia, dating back to the late lower Proterozoic-Neo-Archaean period (>2.5 Ga). Regarded as the extreme southwestern margin of the Congo Craton (a section of the planet's continental crust), the EMC was formed during the first geological

mountain-building process, or orogenesis, known as the Vaalian. The Archaean granitoid gneisses were originally formed between 2,585 and 2,645 Ma – the oldest rocks so far discovered in Namibia. The name Epupa is a Herero word for 'foam', as is created by the cascading water.

The water negotiates a series of ledges in the Kunene River, which changes markedly along its course as it is shaped by many faults and joints. At the falls, the flow is contained within a narrow, deeply incised valley – the result of a tectonic fault – characterized by steeply sloping sides, a straight channel and a narrow floodplain. Here, the river is about 500 m wide and drops in a series of waterfalls spread over 1.5 km, with the greatest single drop being 37 m, before reaching a more trough-shaped watercourse.

For a number of years, the governments of Namibia and Angola have been considering the construction of a hydroelectric dam across the Kunene River – a highly controversial proposal, considering that some of the most important environmental and social impacts have either been excluded or downplayed by environmental impact assessments. By the reports' own admission, some of these impacts are unquantifiable: they include the loss of the Epupa Falls, compromised biodiversity, flooding of ancestral graves and an impact on social environments, including trade and culture – none of whose values can be determined in monetary terms alone.

TIRAS MOUNTAINS

The Mesoproterozoic (1,600–1,000 Ma) was a time of major crust generation within a global accretionary event in which many 'building blocks', called 'cratons', floated together and formed Rodinia, recognized as one of the very first identifiable supercontinents on Earth. This event precipitated the first large-scale mountain-building episodes in Namibia, known as the Vaalian and lower Mokolian orogenies, when the Tiras Mountains were formed. This range consists mainly of the spectacular Tumuab pink granites. Lying at the edge of the Namib Desert (inland from Lüderitz), it forms part of the 'escarpment zone' where semi-desert morphs into savanna. The Tiras Mountains are famous for their lithops, succulent plants that resemble pebbles – only these pebbles are alive!

The majestic, baobab-lined Kunene River banks feature granitoid gneisses that have been polished over the ages by running water. They are part of a vast metamorphic complex in which the characteristics of the original rock formation have been partially erased. However, geologists are able to access and study these rocks in great detail, gleaning information about the extremely old and still poorly understood early history of Nambian geology.

CHAPTER 4

AFRICA'S LARGEST CANYON

It takes a while and some effort to carve a canyon, particularly when it's the Fish River Canyon, which, in terms of size and grandeur, is second only to the Grand Canyon in the United States of America. Time is the master architect of this colossal and rare natural monument, whose layered structure includes some 1,400 million years of Earth's geological history. Across this immense and inconceivable expanse of time, a combination of different processes has been – and still is – at work: weathering (the erosive action of wind, rain, cold, ice, heat, etc.), the transport of sediments by water and wind, and the uplifting forces of tectonic activity have together shaped the geological canyon.

This astonishingly barren and immense landscape provides a snapshot of geological processes that have played out over an unimaginably long period of time.

1.4 BILLION YEARS AGO TO PRESENT

As they dig deep into the Earth's subsurface, canyons reveal extremely old geological layers that would otherwise possibly never be observed. Canyons are therefore valuable repositories of our planet's long history, revealing key facts about the evolution of its environment, glaciation ages, tectonic activity, marine invasions, palaeogeography, constantly mutating climate, and life itself, including its evolution and extinctions.

HOW TO CARVE A CANYON

The Fish River flows more than 650 km across the Namibian plateau from its source east of the Naukluft Mountains to its confluence with the Orange River at the border with South Africa. From about 100 km south of the town of Seeheim, flowing south to Aïs-Aïs, the Fish River has carved a gorge for itself in the Namibian plateau, cutting down as deep as 550 m and as wide as 27 km in places, over a stretch of some 90 km.

The canyon is one of the most impressive geological features of the African continent. A fast-rewind trip all the way back in time, approximately 350 Ma, would reveal a rather flat surface, but one on which water starts seeping and slowly penetrating into a network of fissures and fractures. Over geological time, as the seepage deepens and enlarges channels into the hard rock substrate, a river begins to take shape. The numerous wide meanders reflect that for a considerable period of time this river flowed rather slowly and lazily across flat land towards the sea. This geological phenomenon, where a river maintains its original course despite subsequent uplift or deformation, is known as 'antecedence'.

Another phenomenon then comes into play: over an immense period of time, and extremely slowly, tectonic uplift pushes the whole terrain upwards and tilts it, significantly increasing the surface gradient, while at the same time maintaining the existing geomorphological drainage pattern of the river. This new, steeper topography has the effect of speeding up the rate of flow of the river within its existing river bed, causing it to incise deeper and deeper, all the way down into 1.4 Ga-old layers of terrain on its way to the sea – without ever deviating from the path of its original meander. This geological phenomenon is known as 'superimposition' as it reinforces, in a new geological era, an already existing palaeostructure.

The conjunction of these two geological phenomena – antecedence and superimposition – is what has led to the spectacular Fish River Canyon.

Opposite

Rocks that rise directly above the river bed are ancient gneisses of the Namaqua Metamorphic Complex. They are crowned by the subhorizontal layers of the Nama sediments.

Following pages

A close-up of the Fish River Canyon rock formation shows black dolerite dykes that cross-cut the gneisses of the Namaqua Metamorphic Complex, but not the younger Nama sediments.

A GEOLOGICAL HISTORIAN

The Fish River Basin is located on the western margin of the Kalahari Craton, a stable granitic-gneissic shield that forms the very nucleus of the southern African subcontinent. The Fish River Basin covers an extensive area of southern Namibia, draining an area of about 120,000 km². Because it comprises rocks formed during most of the major rock-forming periods known in Namibia, there is much variety among the rock types, fossils and mineral deposits found here; and the landforms of the basin reflect this variety, as well as the long geomorphological history of the area.

Along its stratified cliffs, the Fish River Canyon majestically exposes one of the longest geological timelines of our planet, lasting some 1.4 Ga, i.e. dating back to even before the primitive Rodinia supercontinent was formed. Its erosive action reveals the multiple layers of the Gondwana supercontinent, which formed approximately 550 Ma, and would later break up into Africa, South America, India, Australia and Antarctica. While

the Fish River was excavating its canyon, it also experienced a number of glaciation eras: three 'snowball' eras and the Dwyka glaciation era, which lasted from 300–200 Ma.

Such glaciation events contributed massively to the further grinding of the canyon, and it was later impacted by the opening of the South Atlantic Ocean 120 Ma.

The canyon has more recently been impacted by the opening of the East African rift (25–22 Ma) and the continuing tectonic uplift of the southern African continent, a phenomenon known as the 'African superswell'.

Over time, through all these successive ages, the Fish River Canyon has undergone many tectonic events, from contraction to stretching, all reflecting extremely complex geodynamic activity.

The wide, meandering course of the canyon follows the original path the river took when it first started flowing on mostly level land sloping gradually to the sea, approximately 350 Ma.

From the main viewpoint, the Fish River Canyon stretches out into the distance, dwarfing the human figure and car atop the Nama Group rock formation that crowns the underlying Namaqua Metamorphic Complex.

UNPACKING THE LAYERS

At its lowest level, the basement of the canyon comprises the Namaqua Metamorphic Complex. Originally this formation was composed of layers of sediments and volcanic rocks deposited some 1.4 Ga. Approximately 1.2 Ga, these layers were intruded by granitic magma and, under high pressures and temperatures, were progressively transformed into metamorphic rocks, i.e. into gneiss, amphibolite, schist and granulite – rocks that can easily be observed today, especially at Aïs-Aïs at the southern end of the Fish River Canyon.

The Rodinia supercontinent started fragmenting 825 Ma, and about 770 Ma the Namaqua Metamorphic Complex was subjected to huge magma injections, which formed dolerite dykes. They are easily recognizable today as they form unmistakable prominent dark intrusions that crisscross the canyon walls.

As tectonic and volcanic activity subsided, a long erosion phase began in the Namaqualand Mountains. It wore down the upper part of the structure, shaping it into a peneplain – a levelled ground surface – around 600 Ma.

This peneplain would in due course be flooded by the marine transgression of the Adamastor Ocean, which opened about 750 Ma and closed again 535 Ma – both events caused by tectonic activity. This marine invasion gave rise to the accumulation of 3,000 m of sediments over the period 550–535 Ma, forming the so-called Nama Group deposits. As no major phase of deformation or metamorphism followed their deposition, the Nama Group deposits are still nearly horizontal today and have preserved their original sedimentary structure, thus forming a sharp contrast to the

monumental underlying Namaqua metamorphic rocks. This geological sequence of marine transgression and retreat left behind a legacy in the rocks: well-preserved and distinctive burrow patterns created by what are presumed to have been worms, named *Treptichnus pedum*. Their burrows, aged 635–541 Ma, have long been considered to be the earliest trace fossils yet found on Earth, until the recent discovery of an older macro-organism, aged 2.1 Ga, in Gabon (published in *Nature*, July 2010).

A GAP IN TIME

There's more than meets the eye in the Fish River Canyon: the traces of some events may have been obliterated, but there's enough evidence to show that they certainly happened.

The Namaqua Metamorphic Complex, which sits at the basement of the Fish River Canyon, comprises some of the oldest rocks in southern Namibia, dating from 1.4–1.05 Ga. The next observable layer is of marine sediments of the Nama Group deposits, dating from 550–535 Ma. Is it possible that during this unimaginably long, 500 Ma gap, nothing happened at all?

We now know that between these two geological ages there was an intermediate phase characterized by fierce and extended erosion that actively weathered the heights of the Namaqua Metamorphic Complex – the upper parts of dykes, together with everything around and above them – as some sharp cuts in the dolerite dykes show. Thus proof of the summit of the Namaqua Metamorphic Complex was simply erased forever. A new sedimentary era, brought in by the marine transgression of the Adamastor and Khomas oceans, built up younger layers on top of the remaining eroded old structure. This gap in the geological record is called a 'discontinuity' or 'unconformity'.

CHAPTER 5

CAVES AND CENOTES

Namibia is the driest country in Africa south of the Sahara – a land of endless sand dunes running into the Atlantic Ocean. It is characterized by a semi-arid to arid climate, with a very limited occurrence of surface water. It is therefore almost entirely reliant on the hidden resource of groundwater, which, fortunately, abounds. Indeed, not everyone knows that it offers opportunities for exceptional freshwater diving! Over the past century, thousands of boreholes have been drilled across the country. Today, some 100,000 boreholes supply enough groundwater to support industrial, rural and municipal water supplies. They provide drinking water for humans, livestock, game and other wildlife, as well as irrigation water for crop production and industrial and mining operations.

The Dragon's Breath Lake is located 46 km northwest of Grootfontein in the northwest of Namibia, and lies about 100 m below the surface. At 170 m x 140 m, it is considered to be the largest non-subglacial underground lake in the world.

© Johnny Bouffartigue

750 MILLION YEARS AGO

KARSTIFICATION

Carbonated terrain, like limestone, can easily be dissolved by rain water, which is acidic. As it runs through fractures and cracks in the rock surface, the water gradually enlarges small gaps and passages and, over geological time, these become larger and larger networks of interconnected conduits and waterways. This water-weathering process, known as 'karstification', slowly carves its way into susceptible terrain, eventually creating underground drainage systems that can be vast. It operates mainly on carbonate rocks – limestone, dolomite (sometimes called 'marble'), but also on evaporates such as gypsum, anhydrite or rock salt. Geologists have classified these affected rocks as the karst group of rocks, and a karst landscape might include features such as caves and caverns, karst depressions, lakes, disappearing streams and springs.

It is estimated that karst landscapes occupy up to 15% of the Earth's land surface, and that as much as a quarter of the world's population is supplied by karst water.

The term 'cenote' comes from the word *ts'onot*, used by the lowland Yucatec Maya. It refers to a natural depression or sinkhole resulting from undermined limestone bedrock, giving access to the groundwater underneath. Cenotes, formed by the same process of water weathering, are defined by the collapse of the cavity roof, either partially, where some rock overhang remains, or entirely, which results in an open pool.

Karst formations are famous worldwide for their scenic beauty, offering almost mystical vistas of grottoes and caves, springs, underground rivers and lakes that excite the imagination and can conjure up notions of fabulous creatures that might live there.

THE MAGIC TRIANGLE OF NAMIBIA

Near the Otavi Mountains in northeastern Namibia, lying between the small towns of Otavi, Tsumeb and Grootfontein, is the 'Golden Triangle', also known as the 'maize triangle': an area of abundant, fresh, clear groundwater. As a consequence, this is the one and only region in Namibia where farmers can grow corn, and in quantities that make it viable to be exported.

The Otavi Mountainland, mostly composed of 750 million-year-old limestone, is 1,300–1,900 m above sea level. In this region of 5,000 km², some of the biggest underground lakes have been discovered quite recently in the limestone and dolomite countryside. For hydrogeologists and speleologists, this is a magic region for exploring caves and sinkholes, up to 140 of which have been documented. Unfortunately, visiting them is not recommended for the general public, as some require highly specialized speleology equipment and considerable practical experience in the field.

Reaching the surface of the Dragon's Breath Lake about 100 m below ground level is only the start of a fantastic adventure. These speleologists aboard their rubber boats illuminate by torchlight just the first few metres of water, the depth of which is unknown.

The Otavi Mountainland area also boasts two large, fully exposed lakes, Otjikoto and Guinas, formed by a pair of neighbouring cenotes. They are both situated on the northern platform of the Damara orogenic belt, which consists predominantly of shelf carbonates that are some 750 Ma. Originally a system of underground caverns and tunnels that became unstable and collapsed, what now remains are circular sinkholes exposed to the open air.

THE GHAUB CAVE (-19.483932°/17.778428°)

The Ghaub Cave is located near Tsumeb, on the nearby Ghaub Guest Farm; it is suitable for visits by the general public, including children, and visits to the site can be arranged at the farm. Discovered early in the 20th century and proclaimed a national monument in 1967, the Ghaub Cave offers a labyrinth of chambers and corridors. It descends 38 m below ground, and visitors can proceed along passages that extend for 2.5 km. At the far end, secluded chambers offer stunning formations that are well worth the effort of crawling through a few narrow sections along the way. The Ghaub Cave is just about the only such feature open to visitors in Namibia, as access to most of the others is limited to professional speleologists. The geological beauty of the Ghaub Cave has in the past unfortunately not been safeguarded – the rock walls have been defaced with graffiti, and stalactites were removed by vandals at a time when access to the cave was not controlled.

DRAGON'S BREATH CAVE (-19.517103°/17.783394°)

The Dragon's Breath Cave – named for the flow of humid air that escapes from its entrance – is located on private land 46 km northwest of Grootfontein in the Otjozondjupa Region. It was discovered in 1986 by members of the South African Speleological Association. A huge underground lake was found at the bottom of the cave, considered to be the largest non-subglacial underground lake in the world. With a diameter of approximately 250 m and a surface area of almost 5 ha, it has an estimated depth of over 100 m, and contains an estimated volume of 5 million m^3 of fresh water. The lake surface is about 80 m below ground level but its bottom has not yet been surveyed. Authorization to explore the cave is required from the farm owner (Sarel Lacante), together with payment of a substantial fee. Access to the abyss is rather difficult, involving a good mastery of speleology practices.

HARASIB CAVE (-19.496889°/17.792861°)

Harasib Cave is a typical cenote, with a partly collapsed roof. It is located just 2.5 km away from Dragon's Breath Cave, on the same farm. It is believed that the waters of both these features could be connected to the large Etosha Pan, some 150 km further north. The particular conditions of the lake at the bottom of the cave – stillness of sediments and stability of temperature – have given rise to one of the world's rarest fish species: the golden cave catfish *(Clarias cavernicola)*, so far found nowhere else.

It took about 3 million years for a small cavity to be transformed into the impressive Ghaub Cave that exists today, and is now a national monument. At the far end of the 2.5 km-long channel, the manager of the Ghaub Guest Farm, Mika (an enthusiastic and friendly cave explorer), takes amazed visitors into this secluded chamber with its flowstone curtains.

OTJIKOTO CENOTE LAKE (-19.194722°/17.549722°)

Otjikoto Lake is probably the most famous permanent lake in Namibia, with remarkable emerald green waters surrounded by vertical limestone cliffs. It was formed when the roof of a huge karst cave collapsed entirely, exposing the lake to the skies. Located 24 km northwest of Tsumeb, it is accessed from the main road B1, *en route* to the Namutoni entrance of the Etosha National Park. The perfectly circular lake has a diameter of 102 m, with a surface of about 7,850 m². Legend has it that the lake is bottomless, or that it is connected to other underground lake systems, including to the neighbouring Lake Guinas; these speculations have not yet been established. Its depth is probably greater than 100 m, and its volume approximately 1 million m³ of fresh water. Its temperature remains steady – 22°C near the surface and 18°C at deeper levels. *Tilapia guinasana*, an endemic, mouth-brooding species of fish that was originally found only in Otjikoto's sister lake, Guinas, has been introduced to Otjikoto Lake for conservation purposes.

When the Herero moved into the area, they named the feature Otjikoto (*otji* in Herero meaning 'deep hole' or 'the place too deep for cattle to drink'). The first Europeans to discover the lake were Briton Francis Galton and Swede Carl Johan Andersson – they happened upon it in 1851 while on a mission to find Lake Ngami in Botswana, north of the Kalahari Desert. Upon spotting the lake, the two explorers immediately jumped in for a swim. The local people could hardly believe what they

Otjikoto Lake, northwest of Tsumeb, shines like a gem in the arid Namibian landscape and illustrates the phenomenon of groundwater having become surface water.

were witnessing – that these two individuals could safely swim back to shore, contrary to the local belief that no-one would survive immersion in the lake's mysterious waters.

Otjikoto Lake featured in an incident that occurred towards the end of World War I. When German troops *(Schutztruppe)* in the vicinity of Otjikoto were forced to surrender to forces of the British Union of South Africa in June 1915, instead of conceding their weapons to the enemy, they dumped their artillery, heavy guns and even ammunition wagons into the lake. Much of the dumped war material has now been recovered, although it is rumoured that a large safe filled with 6 million gold Deutsche Mark coins is still sitting at the bottom of the lake, its edges and keyhole sealed with molten lead. Only a long-held fear restrains many fortune hunters from venturing into the lake: to add to the local inhabitants' original fears, the ghost of a German soldier who drowned in the emerald green depths is said to haunt its waters. Salvaged war material, including an ammunition wagon in perfect condition, can be viewed at the Alte Feste Museum in Windhoek. Restored cannons and other arms are also displayed in the nearby Tsumeb Museum.

Cave-diving fans, on the other hand, are not in the least intimidated by legends: Otjikoto Lake is now one of the premier dive sites in Namibia, as on-site development shows: stairs have been installed down the vertical rock wall, as well as a diving platform at the water's edge and a winch to carry diving equipment down and up again.

GUINAS CENOTE LAKE (-19.232918°/17.352650°)

Lake Guinas, known to the San as Gaisis ('ugly' in the Herero language), is situated southwest of its sister lake Otjikoto, a 50-km round trip from the main road B1. The detour to Lake Guinas is well worth the extra driving as the lake is not only deeper and clearer, it is much more scenic (in spite of the San description) than its more frequently visited neighbour. Lake Guinas' extremely clear waters are of a rare and intense cobalt blue colour. The lake is elliptical in shape, with a surface area of 118 m x 62 m (5,750 m^2). At 130 m deep, it contains approximately 600,000 m^3 of fresh water. The temperature throughout the body of water is constant all year at 26°C; this, together with good visibility, makes Lake Guinas an ideal choice of dive site. On 13 May 2001, South African Trevor Hutton set a world record here in free-diving, of 66 m in 2 minutes and 11 seconds.

Lake Guinas is the natural home of *Tilapia guinasana*, a beautiful, 14 cm-long, golden fish. Tilapias are found around the rocky walls of the lake, where they establish their breeding territories. South African Verna van Schaik, who holds the world record for the deepest dive by a woman, recalls her dives into Lake Guinas as 'some of the most stunning dives [I have] ever done. The walls of the lake are covered in multi-coloured fish, creating a jewelled and entertaining landscape. In fact, the fish [are] literally everywhere: even at one hundred and ten metres shoals of silver still accompanied [me] as [I] swam ever deeper into a huge unexplored and seemingly endless cavern.'

FOSSILS AND FOOTPRINTS

CHAPTER 6

FOSSILS AND FOOTPRINTS

Palaeontology is the study of the living forms of past geological times, based on the fossilized remains of plants and animals. A relatively recent science, dating from the early 20th century, palaeontology enables the reconstruction of vanished living environments and the lines of descent of living beings across numerous mass exctinctions that have occurred throughout history. Fossils are, therefore, passports to exploring the ancient history of our world.

Stepping into dinosaurs' footprints on the Etjo Sandstone Formation (dated 190 Ma) can transport one back to the days of the popular movie, *Jurassic Park*. These tridactyl marks belonged to a theropod dinosaur that wandered in the area well before it was named the Otjihaenamaparero Farm in the 20th century. The site is located northeast of Omaruru.

750–190 MILLION YEARS AGO

For most city-dwellers, fossils can be viewed at natural history museums, lined up on dusty shelves under dimmed lights, and described on yellowing labels. But for the inquisitive traveller, there remain a few places on Earth where fossils still show up in the wild, exactly where they were once deposited, and where they have lain untouched for millions of years. Namibia is one of these extraordinary lands – a paradise for serious palaeontologists and fossil enthusiasts. Namibia is indeed an interesting place, both geologically and palaeontologically speaking, where a number of ancient milestones can be identified. Here, the visible remains of our history start during the Gondwanaland era some 750 Ma.

STROMATOLITES (750–700 Ma)

Stromatolite fossils are solid, layered structures produced in shallow water by marine bacterial activity – that of single-celled microbes called 'cyanobacteria' (blue-green algae) – in the form of microbial mats. Stromatolites are, in a way, the fossilized equivalent of old reefs. These structures were once numerous in the shallow waters of the ancient Damara Ocean between the Congo Craton in the north and the Kalahari Craton in the south, some 750 Ma; they developed a layer 5,000 m thick – now mostly eroded – over a distance of 100 km along the current Otavi Mountainland (the triangular area described by the towns Otavi, Tsumeb and Grootfontein).

Some stromatolites have survived to this day, in a range of environments. They can be found in the ocean at Shark Bay in Australia and in freshwater lakes around the globe. The oldest stromatolite fossil yet found – in Isua, Greenland – has been dated at 3.8 Ga. It is possible that no older stromatolites remain to be found, as before that, the massive meteoritic bombardment that struck Earth between its formation in 4.5 Ga and 4 Ga probably destroyed any and all traces of life.

Stromatolites can be found in many locations in Namibia, such as the Otavi Mountainland, Hiker's Point in the Fish River Canyon and, with particularly easy access, at the Otjitotongwe Cheetah Guest Farm near Kamanjab.

MESOSAURUS (280–248 Ma)

The Mesosaurus Inland Sea formed on the Gondwana continent between what is today the split up Congo Craton in the north, the Kalahari Craton in the south, South America and Antarctica. This sea was most probably entirely enclosed or in contact with the world ocean Panthalassa through only a few, narrow seaways. If the water of

This vertical cross section shows colonies of unbranched, parallel, columnar growth structured stromatolites, such as are seen in the Otavi Mountainland in central Namibia. They are thought to have formed under the influence of marine microbial mats that trap and bind particulate sediment and enhance cementation.

the Mesosaurus Inland Sea was initially saline, it gradually turned brackish before becoming fresh, thanks to the river systems flowing into the restricted basin. This sea is named after the small swimming vertebrate, *Mesosaurus*, that inhabited it for a short time in the early Permian, and existed nowhere else on Earth.

Because fossils of the *Mesosaurus* reptile were found on both sides of the Atlantic Ocean – in southern Africa and South America – they provided key evidence to support the theory of continental drift, proposed by geophysicist Alfred Wegener in the first half of the 20th century.

Mesosaurus resembled a lizard, with a long, narrow head and its nostrils situated high up on the snout, near the eyes. It therefore had only to break the surface of the water in order to breathe and see. The pointed snout sported long, thin, pin-like teeth on elongated jaws. It can be presumed that these teeth were not strong enough to bite

This *Mesosaurus* fossil was found by Giel Steenkamp on his farm, Spitzkop, better known as Mesosaurus Fossil Camp, in southern Namibia. This freshwater reptile had a long, narrow skull and an extended tail; its ribs were robust, probably reinforcing the ribcage for long dives.

Over time, stromatolites silicified (silicification being a major process of fossilization) so that they were harder than the surrounding sedimentary rock structure that gradually built up around them. After weathering of the surrounding rock, the stromatolites remain nearly untouched and still today show up in relief.

prey, but were rather used to filter algae and soft-bodied organisms or small, krill-like crustaceans from the water. Because it was an aquatic animal, its short forelegs and longer hind legs were most probably equipped with webbed feet. The tail and hind legs propelled the animal through the water, while the forelegs were used for steering. *Mesosaurus* could easily flex from side to side, an adaptation common in water-dwelling vertebrates.

Mesosaurus fossils can be seen on site at the Mesosaurus Fossil Camp and Quiver Tree Dolerite Park, which are both about 20 km east of Giant's Playground, itself located some 20 km northeast of Keetmanshoop. At these sites, owners Giel and Hendrik Steenkamp take visitors to explore their fossil wonderland.

THE KHORIXAS PETRIFIED FOREST (280 MA)

There are traces of trees in Namibia, aged about 280 Ma, that were adapted to a cold climate and grew at the edge of glaciers, as they do in today's Alaska and Siberia. These traces can still be seen today.

The Khorixas Petrified Forest, 45 km west of Khorixas in Damaraland, is a deposit of large, fossilized tree trunks, believed to be the remnants of extensive woodlands that once covered the land. The fact that the trunks were found lying parallel to each other within fluvial sediments suggests that they were swept away from their original location and carried, possibly over some distance, by an event such as a glacial outburst flood. This event would have happened in the Permian age during brutal climate change at the end of a 'snowball Earth' period, and bears testimony to a significant climatic disaster where forces at work were able to sweep away an entire forest of some 30 m-high trees, and deposit the logs elsewhere, possibly several thousand metres away. One of the trunks, 30 m in extent, has been identifed as an ancestor of one of today's conifers – the *Araucaria*.

Remnants of this ancient forest, now spread over several tens of square kilometres, constitute the most important deposit of petrified trees in southern Africa.

DINOSAUR FOOTPRINTS OF OTJIHAENAMAPARERO (190 MA)

The Aeolian Sandstone Formation of Etjo was formed 190 Ma in the Karoo age, during the Early Jurassic period. In those times, central Namibia was covered by lakes and thick vegetation, a situation that lasted several millions of years, and that provided a perfect platform for dinosaurs. But gradually the climate changed, and humidity dropped. As winds blew across the partly denuded flats, the lakes

Today, 280 million years later, we can walk alongside the petrified remains of a long-lost forest in Damaraland that probably fell victim to a climatic event in which 30 m-high trees were ripped from the ground and dumped far from where they had grown.

filled with sand and became mere wetlands. Dinosaurs adapted to this harsh new environment in which waterholes were scarce, and occasional rainfall fed what were now ephemeral lakes and rivers. Creatures that came to drink left their footprints in the damp sediment at the water's edge. The impressions were quickly filled by new layers of sediment, blown in by the winds. Over millions of years, the layers of sand hardened into the Etjo Sandstone Formation, thus protecting the footprints from erosion and damage. Gradually, as climatic conditions changed and geological forces triggered phases of erosion, the overlying layers were worn down until the buried tracks were revealed.

A remarkable variety of vertebrate fossils has been found in the Mesozoic rocks of the Omingonde and Etjo formations. Herbivores of various sizes and the large carnivore *Erythrosuchus africanus* frequented the lake shore and river flats during the Triassic (c. 220 Ma), while *Massospondylus* of the infraorder Prosauropoda, a herbivore of 3–5 m in length and 1.5 m in height, lived in the interdune valleys of the early Etjo period, some 200 Ma. Preserved skeletal parts of *Massospondylus* have been removed from their place of discovery, and casts have been made of impressions left in the rock, and these relics are on display at the National Earth Science Museum in Windhoek, which also features a life-size reconstruction of this creature.

Dinosaur footprints can still be seen *in situ* at various locations, the most famous being on the farm Otjihaenamaparero at the foot of Klein Etjo, some 65 km northeast of Omaruru. At this location, where two pathways intersect, more than 30 footprints can be identified, many of the individual tracks measuring approximately 45 x 35 cm, with a stride of some 70–90 cm. These tracks clearly indicate three-toed, clawed feet, and their arrangement suggests they were made by the hind feet of a bipedal animal. Unfortunately, no body fossils have been found in the area so far, and one is therefore limited to using comparisons with other tracks for identification. From the few dozen footprints that have been discovered and identified round the world, the imprints made by the Otjihaenamaparero dinosaur suggest that it belonged to a large carnivorous theropod species, and most likely to the family of the Ceratosauria – the earliest known highly specialized meat-eaters. About 3 m in length, Ceratosaurians had very strong hind limbs that may have allowed them to run as fast as 40 km/h while maintaining a very narrow gait, with the body forward and the tail held out nearly horizontally behind them as a counterbalance.

Some lesser tracks were probably made by the small Ceratosaurian *Syntarsus*, which was about the size of a secretarybird, and lived and hunted in flocks. It was a ferocious predator, and built for speed.

Other tracks from the Etjo Formation at Waterberg have been linked to *Massospondylus* and two other Prosauropod dinosaurs: the bipedal *Quemetrisauropus princeps*, and the four-legged *Prototrisauropus crassidiitus*, which had massive, long-tailed bodies and could grow to a length of 7 m and 10 m, respectively. Both herbivores, they had relatively small heads and very long necks that enabled them to browse on plants high above the ground.

Tracks of cynodonts also occur in the area. They have been attributed to *Tritylodon* and *Pachygenelus*. Both were advanced cynodonts: *Tritylodon* had a very mammal-like lower jaw and complex post-canine teeth that would have enabled it to crush and slice food. It was so mammal-like that it was initially classified as such. The similar *Pachygenelus* was slightly larger, and both animals were herbivorous. They may well have served as prey for the carnivorous dinosaurs of the time.

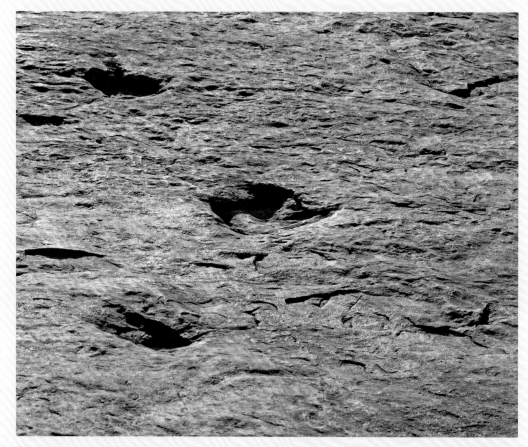

These Precambrian-age rocks are inconceivably old, and yet they and their trace fossils can still be found today. The secret to their preservation over such a vast span of time is their burial deep in the Earth, where they have been protected from erosion, but where they have also been heated and deformed – metamorphosed – by pressure.

Following pages

Lesser flamingos move lightly along the Atlantic Ocean shore where air, sea and sand dunes meet, creating an awe-inspiring sight.

CHAPTER 7

SNOWBALL EARTH

NASA's Cassini spacecraft recently beamed back to Earth some dazzling photographs of Saturn's moon, Enceladus, which has a small diameter of just 505 km. A bright, white moon that is entirely covered in ice, Enceladus is regarded by planetary explorers as the most reflective body in the solar system. But there have been larger icy celestial bodies in our solar system before: the Earth happens to have been one of them, when its entire surface – both the continents and oceans – was covered in ice. From the Moon, Earth must have looked very much the way Enceladus appears from the Cassini spacecraft: like a giant snowball, and hence the popular name of the theory, 'snowball Earth'.

These deeply eroded limestones, indicative of a 'snowball Earth' episode, are found north of the Divorce Pass along the Doros Crater 4x4 trail in the Dorob National Park in western Namibia. Their presence has revealed the existence of cap carbonates – continuous layers of limestone that are distinct from standard carbonates, and which serve as markers of past glacial events in today's hot, deserted landscape.

630 MILLION YEARS AGO

SNOWBALL EARTH

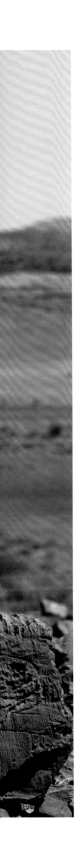

The 'snowball' phenomenon has impacted Earth several times since its first known episode c. 2.45 Ga. Such radically significant climate changes could have been triggered by a range of different factors, some relating to the inner structure of Earth itself (tectonic and volcanic activity), some being astronomical and others even extraterrestrial.

Although the extent of glaciation around equatorial regions during snowball Earth events is still fiercely debated among scientists, significant glacial events irrefutably happened during this geological timespan, with evidence of glacial deposits of a similar age having been found in widely scattered regions all around the globe. Proof of such events is clearly visible in Namibia today.

SNOWBALL EARTH HYPOTHESIS

The snowball Earth hypothesis was first formulated by Joseph Kirschvink from the California Institute of Technology, or Caltech, in 1992. The theory was amplified in 1998 in an article by Paul Hoffman from Harvard University, published in the journal *Science*, in which he presented new evidence from Namibia, showing that ice extended to near equatorial latitudes in the late Precambrian (about 700 Ma). Although deeper regions of the sea may have remained liquid during snowball Earth episodes, icebergs or thick ice sheet to depths of 1,500 m would indisputably have covered all the oceans. Earth's temperature would have then dropped to between -20 and -50°C.

The fact is that glaciations leave evidence wherever they have occurred: a characteristic topography results, showing grooves and scratches ground by glaciers passing over hard rocks. And, perhaps more tellingly, glacial debris (palaeo-moraine) is left behind, such as tillites or diamictite, and dropstones, which are rocks that have been transported long distances by icebergs and then dropped where and when the ice has melted, far away from their place of origin. Tillite deposits have been found in virtually all latitudes of the globe, including regions located at the equator at those times. Their presence can be interpreted as the physical proof that glaciation extended to near-equatorial latitudes, in contrast to the more recent glaciations that extended from the poles to mid-latitudes only.

A snowball Earth event can be triggered by multiple factors:

- Astronomical cycles – disruptions of Earth's orbit or axial tilt (obliquity) – could precipitate such an event. As Earth heads towards the furthest point from the Sun on its elliptical orbit, it receives less and less solar energy, causing temperatures on Earth to drop dramatically. Known as 'Milankovitch cycles', these perturbations could initiate a glaciation event.

Along the hard and bumpy dirt track from the Messum Crater, heading north to the Doros Crater, geology transforms the old mineral roots of the continent into postmodern sculptures. In recent times, the landscape has been carved by erosion as acid rain dissolves the limestones.

- Exceptional volcanic activity could start a so-called 'volcanic long winter' during which temperatures fall to extremely low negative values: triggers could be a supervolcano eruption, mantle plume activity, or traps eruptions (in which substantial fields of lava spread out over an area, giving rise to a vast igneous province).
- A major meteorite impact can initiate an 'impact winter', where the atmosphere is filled with ash that prevents sunlight from reaching the Earth.
- Tectonic activity endlessly repositions the continents on the Earth's surface. When several continents aggregate, they together form a supercontinent (e.g. Rodinia or Gondwana). If such a supercontinent happens to be positioned at an equatorial latitude, a huge region of Earth's crust is suddenly subject to heavy rainfall, dramatically increasing erosion on the planet. This erosion process consumes and captures large quantities of carbon dioxide (CO_2) from the atmosphere, decreasing the greenhouse effect and replacing it with an ice-house effect. Without the greenhouse effect, Earth's average temperature would be approximately -18°C, as opposed to our current average temperature of 15°C.
- Once Earth has succumbed to the snowball Earth effect, the brilliant white ice sheet covering the globe reflects the Sun's heat, reinforcing the situation, known as 'ice-albedo feedback'.

During a snowball Earth event, dramatic modifications of Earth's crust, oceans and atmosphere would happen simultaneously (albeit over geological times of millions of years):
- Erosion from wind and rain would cease, given that the Earth's crust would no longer be exposed to them.
- As bacterial activity and photosynthesis gradually ceased, oxygen production would be curtailed.
- Oceans covered with ice sheet would suddenly be deprived of oxygen, becoming anoxic, with the result that iron would become soluble in sea water.

Volcanism, however, remains active. With subglacial eruptions continuing under the icecap and ice sheet, they would produce masses of CO_2, which would break through the ice sheet and progressively concentrate in the atmosphere. When this concentration reaches approximately 400 times its present value, it induces a massive new greenhouse effect, which would start melting the ice.

Since deposition of these carbonaceous rocks at the time of 'snowball Earth', massive pressures have not only tilted horizontal planes until they are vertical, but have also transformed smooth rock surfaces into wrinkled old skins.

- As oceans are freed from the ice sheet and Earth's crust re-emerges, the snowball effect is reversed:
- Erosion of silicates begins again and starts trapping and consuming excess amounts of atmospheric CO_2 into specific carbonates, named 'cap carbonates'.
- Earth again becomes oxygenated through bacterial reactivation and photosynthesis. Consequently, iron, which had previously dissolved in the oceans, is brutally precipitated and forms a specific rock material named Banded Iron Formation, or BIF.

The presence of the three sequential geological layers – of tillite deposits, cap carbonates and BIF – is the foundation of the snowball Earth theory.

The first known snowball Earth episode, the Huronian global glaciations, began about 2.45 Ga. Three other episodes occurred between 900 Ma and 580 Ma: Kaigas at c. 750–720 Ma, Sturtian at c. 716 Ma, and Marinoan at c. 635 Ma.

LOOKING FOR SNOWBALL EARTH IN NAMIBIA

There are several spots of geological evidence of snowball Earth in Namibia, although most are in remote and relatively inaccessible places.

- Neoproterozoic glacial deposits and cap carbonates are found in the succession of the Namibian Otavi Group, within the 220 m-thick Rasthof Formation. Marine tillite from the younger Cryogenian glaciation (Ghaub Formation) is found in the same Otavi Group.
- Dropstones, released by the melting ice, can be seen at Great Bay and at Klein Bogenfels.
- At Omutirapo, also in northern Namibia, a 2 km-wide, 400 m-deep palaeo valley is filled with glaciogenic strata of the Chuos Formation, which records the Sturtian glacial occurrence.
- The lower layer of cap carbonate of the Rasthof Formation overlies Neoproterozoic glacial deposits (Chuos Formation) and is exposed in the Khowarib-Warmquelle area in northern Namibia.
- Southern Namibia incorporates at least four Neoproterozoic diamictites (tillites) that can be matched to the Kaigas, Sturtian, Marinoan and Vingerbreek glacial events.

Some geological formations are truly awe-inspiring: titanic terrestrial forces and unimaginably long periods of time have crafted impressive landscapes, smashing the rock structure to pieces and creating paving stones for giants from sheets of limestone.

CHAPTER 8

VOLCANOES AT WORK

A little-known fact is that Namibia is a volcanic land, having been shaped into the landscape we know today by major volcanic and plutonic episodes. Volcanism and plutonism are two different expressions of the same generic phenomenon, magmatism. Volcanism is the name given to magma emissions onto the surface (magma is called 'lava' at this stage) and plutonism is the name given to magma intrusions that remain trapped inside the crust and are unable to reach the surface.

This iconic landscape of the Etendeka Plateau in the Kunene region in northwestern Damaraland rests today in total silence under a cerulean sky. But 131 million years ago it staged one of the largest and most violent volcanic eruptions known on Earth.

580–550 AND 139–128 MILLION YEARS AGO

A major magmatic event stands out in the geological history of Namibia: the Gondwana amalgamation, which was triggered 540 million years ago by the tectonic welding together of the Congo Craton in the north and the Kalahari Craton in the south. During the titanic collision of the two cratons 580–550 Ma, major volcanic and plutonic events forced up a massive mountain range several thousand metres high, similar to the height of the Andes. Over subsequent millions of years this high mountain chain was entirely wiped out by erosion, but we still know it today as the Damara Belt: a central zone, NNE-SSW oriented, approximately 400 km wide and 650 km long. It comprises about one-third of Namibia's current surface and divides the country diagonally in two. Crossing this extended flat area today means venturing 'under the volcano' – 'inside' what used to be an active plutonic layer of the Earth. The realisation gives rise to a shivering sensation!

Even if traces of this major historical event are not easy to recognize with the naked eye, one can certainly find remains of other huge magmatic events in Namibia: LIPs (Large Igneous Provinces), volcanoes, calderas, craters, dyke swarms and magma intrusions, among others.

THE ETENDEKA LARGE IGNEOUS PROVINCE

There are about 18 Large Igneous Provinces (LIPs) on Earth that cover vast areas of the globe. They are composed of massive accumulations of both igneous (or plutonic) and volcanic rocks that were formed by successive gigantic magmatic pulses. Every pulse produced volumes of 1,000–10,000 km³ of magma and lava. The events also released unprecedented amounts of volcanic gas and ash into the atmosphere, reaching up to tens of kilometres in altitude, and sometimes triggering major climate change that resulted in mass extinctions. Single magmatic episodes could last for periods of 10,000 years, while the total duration of an LIP formation could take up to 1 million years. Fortunately, humans have never experienced such catastrophic events.

One of the most violent volcanic eruptions known in Earth's history happened within the gigantic igneous province of Paraná-Etendeka (northwestern Namibia). It took place during the early Cretaceous, 139–128 Ma, at a time when the South Atlantic

Opposite
Growing amid the chaos on a dolerite-strewn hill, Quiver Trees *(Aloe Dichotoma)* reach out to the night sky, throwing their starry leaves into the Milky Way. Although dolerite is chemically similar to basalt, it is rock that has failed to reach the surface and remained trapped underground in networks of fissures until millions of years later, when endless weathering finally exposes it.

Following pages
Namibia certainly offers some of the most unusual walks on Earth, such as here, along the crest of a dolerite injection – a huge black dyke that formed at roughly the same time as the opening of the South Atlantic Ocean some 134 Ma. This formation occurs some 100 km north of Lüderitz.

Ocean was opening up. It is estimated that 6,340 km^3 of magma flowed onto the surface during this phenomenal volcanic episode, burying the region under 2,000 m of lava, of which about 880 m are still in place today. Such a volume would correspond to a magma chamber 23 km in diameter. With the opening of the South Atlantic Ocean, the larger part of this huge LIP was pushed away as part of today's South America, where the Paraná lava field covers an area of at least 1.5 million km^2 over southern Brazil, Uruguay, eastern Paraguay and northern Argentina. The Etendeka part of the LIP, which remained in southern Africa, is just a small remnant, approximately 5% of the total area, and consists of an estimated area of 78,000 km^2 of volcanic rock.

Volcanologists speculate that the eruption process took place over a span of less than a million years. Great volumes of acid rocks were ejected as a result of huge explosive activity and pyroclastic density currents, which are gravity-driven mixtures of magma and gas emitted during explosive eruptions. Such currents are extremely mobile, for they can travel at speeds of up to 700 km/h, at temperatures up to 700°C, and can cover hundreds of kilometres. Nothing escapes these lethal outpourings.

The Etendeka Plateau in northwestern Namibia covers a region of some 78,000 km^2, with the main outcrop located between Cape Cross in the southwest and Sesfontein, incorporating Palmwag, the Goboboseb Mountains and Messum Complex. The landscape is characterized by high, table-topped mountains, hence the Himba name for the area, *Etendeka*, meaning 'the place of flat-topped mountains'. Today, the main lava field (one of many covering the Etendeka Plateau) covers approximately 12,000 km^2, from the Huab River in the south to the Hoanib River in the north.

GIANT DYKE SWARMS

Giant Dyke Swarms (GDS), which generally appear within very old geological formations, have been detected not only on Earth but also on other planets within the solar system, such as Mars and Venus. On Earth, Namibia is one of the very best places to observe them.

At times of great geodynamic activity, like the opening of the South Atlantic Ocean, pressurized magma violently fractures the crust, while simultaneously injecting

Opposite, top and bottom
At Giant's Playground, dolerite 'figures' abound, standing strong and tall like intimidating guardians of the volcanic treasures of Namibia.

Following pages
Some striking encounters can happen amid the rolling sand dunes of the Namib Desert. Here, close to Spencer Bay, a lonely jackal pauses, while behind him a thick band of dolerite – appearing as a charcoal stroke across the mountains – scars the landscape.

The empty and silent Messum Crater to the northeast of Cape Cross is home to many species of beautiful and fragile lichens that slowly grow on the rocks. This crater marks the location (135–132 Ma) of a hotspot that fed a massive volcanic eruption, part of the violent process that created the gigantic igneous province of Paraná-Etendeka.

itself through subsurface fractures, forming dykes. Some dykes reach the surface, generating volcanic eruptions, while some do not and form intrusive bodies. During such subsurface injection episodes, hundreds of cubic kilometres of dolerite are almost instantly forced through dykes that may be many kilometres long, several tens of metres wide and at aeroplane-like speeds of about 700 km/h.

Giant Dyke Swarms are composed of a network of dykes. The presence of such a network is proof of extremely powerful geodynamic activity having taken place. Giant dykes typically exceed 30 m in width and 100 km in length; some can even be 100 m wide and several thousand kilometres long.

Dolerite is the name given to magma that has not reached the surface and has crystallized just below the crust. Most of the dykes that can be seen in Namibia today are dolerite dykes, millions of years of weather having eroded the top layers of crust that had originally buried them. They can appear as striking black lines that run across mountain slopes, sometimes extending through whole mountain ranges. When the country – or host – rock that surrounded them has been totally eroded, they appear as a chaotic pile of huge dolerite blocks.

The Henties Bay-Outjo dyke swarm in northwestern Namibia, a Paraná-Etendeka-related dyke, presents a well-exposed example of the magma feeder system for Large Igneous Provinces. Extending some 400 km inland from the present coastline, and more than 100 km across, the Henties Bay-Outjo dyke swarm contains over 1,000 individual dykes.

Visually stunning giant dyke swarms can be seen at Giant's Playground on the Gariganus farm 13 km northeast of Keetmanshoop, as well as at the Mesosaurus Fossil Camp nearby.

This is a perfect example of symbiosis of totally different organisms – of a fungus and an alga – that results in the formation of lichens. For the past 400 million years lichens have developed on and graced all sorts of substrates in some of the most extreme environments. In arid Namibia, the tenuous survival of these primitive plants is dependent on what is virtually the only source of humidity: the early morning fog and dew.

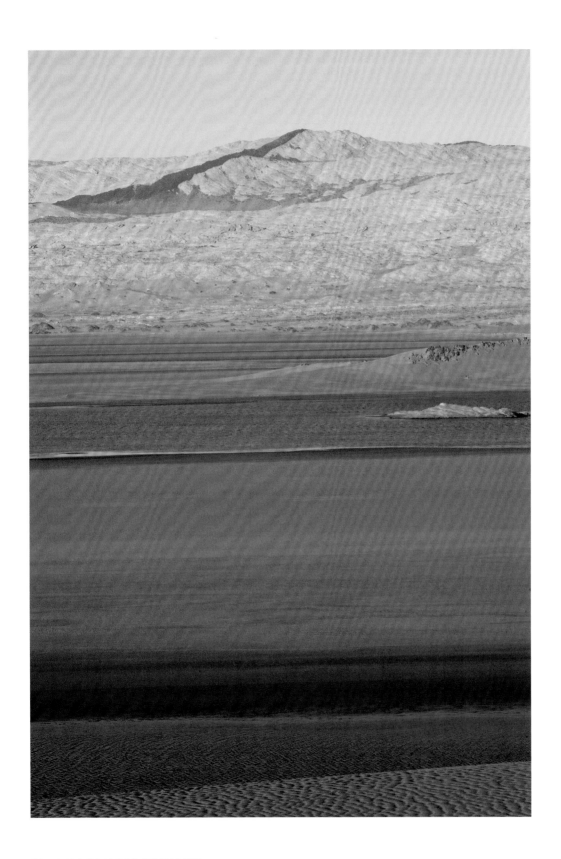

THE MESSUM CRATER

The Messum Crater is an 18 km-diameter, roughly circular volcanic crater to the northeast of Cape Cross. Although the structure is extremely eroded, it can nevertheless be recognized in the field. Volcanic rocks still cover the bottom of the crater, while highly eroded plutonic rocks (gabbro and granites) surround it. A rhyolitic lava dome is visible, forming the central hill.

Driving across the vast and silent crater today gives an overwhelming feeling of emptiness, but also of calm. It is hard to imagine that 135–132 Ma this was the location of a huge hotspot that fed the Paraná-Etendeka LIP, as some geologists believe.

THE BRUKKAROS COMPLEX

The Brukkaros Complex rises some 500–600 m above the surrounding Namaland plain, at the southern edge of the Gibeon Kimberlite-Carbonatite Province, dating from the Upper Cretaceous, about 71.5 Ma. This is no common geological structure: it looks like a volcano with a crater and a rim, but there are no traces of lava rocks anywhere near it! The strange configuration made it quite a mystery; it was even thought that the crater may have been formed by the impact of the Gibeon meteorite. The explanation was finally found, and the crater, along with its surrounding ejecta ring, bears the rather uncommon name of 'maar'.

Maars are formed by explosive eruptions caused by groundwater superheated by magma. As superheated water turns to gas, it erupts at the surface, throwing the host rock into the air, and forming large, deep holes in the ground, called 'diatremes' – volcanic pipes formed by gaseous explosions. When only superheated groundwater causes the explosion of steam, ash and rock, the eruption is termed 'phreatic'; when magma is also part of the blast, it is called 'phreatomagmatic'. Both are 'hydromagmatic' eruptions, i.e. induced by water.

During long, active volcanic episodes, such eruptive processes may occur repeatedly. After each explosion, surface- and groundwater refill the diatreme through the breccias – rocks composed of broken fragments and cemented together by a fine-grained matrix. As each new eruptive explosion occurs, the existing diatreme widens and deepens. Some diatremes have been recorded as up to 2,000 m deep.

Instead of dolerite, maar-diatremes are sometimes composed of kimberlite – magma that originates in the mantle, at depths of 150–200 km, and which is known to carry diamonds. Unfortunately, despite the fact that more than 100 dykes and 74 diatremes have been located in the Brukkaros Complex Field, no diamonds have been found there.

A band of dolerite cuts across a rock formation rising above the golden flats of the Namib Desert's sand dunes, and lapped by the ocean – a scene that encapsulates Namibia's pristine wilderness.

VALLEY OF THE ORGAN PIPES

An example of geological 'jewellery' stands at the foot of a winding road 6 km east of Twyfelfontein: an outcrop of crystallized dolerite columns looking much like an assembly of organ pipes. They are part of a sill that was formed by intruding Damaran and Karoo sediments during magmatic activity related to the break-up of Gondwana in the Early Cretaceous. Unable to reach the surface by cutting vertically through existing host rock, molten magma penetrated horizontally into the surrounding rocks. Because it was trapped under the Earth's surface, the molten dolerite cooled and solidified very slowly, allowing polygonal structures to form. These structures slowly built up into columnar shapes, perpendicular to the surface. The cooling process of magma starts from the edges of the intrusion, moving inwards, so that the polygonal columns build from both top and bottom and meet in the middle, where the magma cools more slowly.

Hexagons make up the geometric pattern that forms naturally during the contraction and shrinking of any soft structure subject to drying or cooling. Similar patterns can be observed on mud flats after rain, when the drying clay forms a pattern of cracks. As these cracks penetrate deeper into the cooling mass, they tend to arrange themselves at 120° to one another, and hexagonal columns result, which minimize heat loss and cooling tensions. However, because there is some randomness in this process, five-sided or seven-sided columns may also be produced.

Above and opposite

The so-called 'Organ Pipes' near Twyfelfontein – regularly shaped copper-coloured dolerite columns that rise to different heights – certainly deserve their name.

CHAPTER 9

WUSTENQUELL'S GRANITE DOMES

Until a few years ago, the natural wonders on Wustenquell Guest Farm were among the best-kept secrets in Namibia, shared among a happy few by word of mouth only. But stories of the jaw-dropping, mind-boggling beauty of the area's naturally sculpted rocks spread, and the site has became so popular that visitors to Namibia these days routinely make a detour to Wustenquell.

Namibian wildlife appears everywhere, even finding form in the solid rock at Wustenquell's Domes! This profile of a granite lion has been dramatically carved by corrasion – the combined action of wind and sand at work over millions of years. These extraordinary rocks have formed at the edge of the Namib-Naukluft National Park in central Namibia.

550 MILLION YEARS AGO

'Tafoni' are granitic erosion forms, superb examples of which can be seen at Wustenquell. Visitors to the area often remark on the seeming portrayal of hauntingly figurative human skulls.

Following pages

This mineral outcrop naturally emerged from below the surface and was then subjected to the powerful sculpting action of wind and sands. The resulting structure would be unimaginable by even the most creative and avant-garde architects!

Resembling the skull of an ancient giant resting in peace, this tafoni 'sculpture' seems almost to have been carved by humans, rather than by ongoing corrasion.

On the edge of the Namib-Naukfuft National Park, Wustenquell's geological wonders come in the form of spectacularly eroded granites. Granites are plutonic rocks that were formed inside the Earth's crust at a time of active surface volcanism. The very slow cooling of the magma (from thousands to hundreds of thousands of years) that was trapped deep below the surface enabled the formation of large crystals – often so big that they can be seen with the naked eye. Over geological time, erosion stripped away thick layers of surface crust until the buried granites were finally unearthed. Despite the inherent hardness of granite, its structure and geomorphology, once exposed to the weathering processes (such as running water, waves, wind, temperature change, glaciers), starts being altered.

TAFONI SCULPTURES

The particular granitic erosion forms at Wustenquell are called 'tafoni' (from the Corsican word *tafone*, meaning 'cavity') – giant, honeycombed, cavernous structures. They belong to the Salem-type granitic suite, aged about 550 million years. Geomorphological features incorporating clusters of hollows (known as 'alveoli'), and reminiscent of Swiss cheese, develop in areas where water or humidity has carved into the rock surface, loosening the crystalline grains of the granite structure. Once formed, the alveoli keep evolving and growing as a result of thermo-cryoclasty (also known as 'freeze-thaw weathering', from alternating cold and hot temperatures), and eventually salt weathering. Over time, tafoni may develop into impressive arches and caverns of several cubic metres, as can be seen at Wustenquell.

 The second and major weathering factor at work at Wustenquell is wind corrasion – the abrasive action of solid materials like silica (sand) and small minerals transported

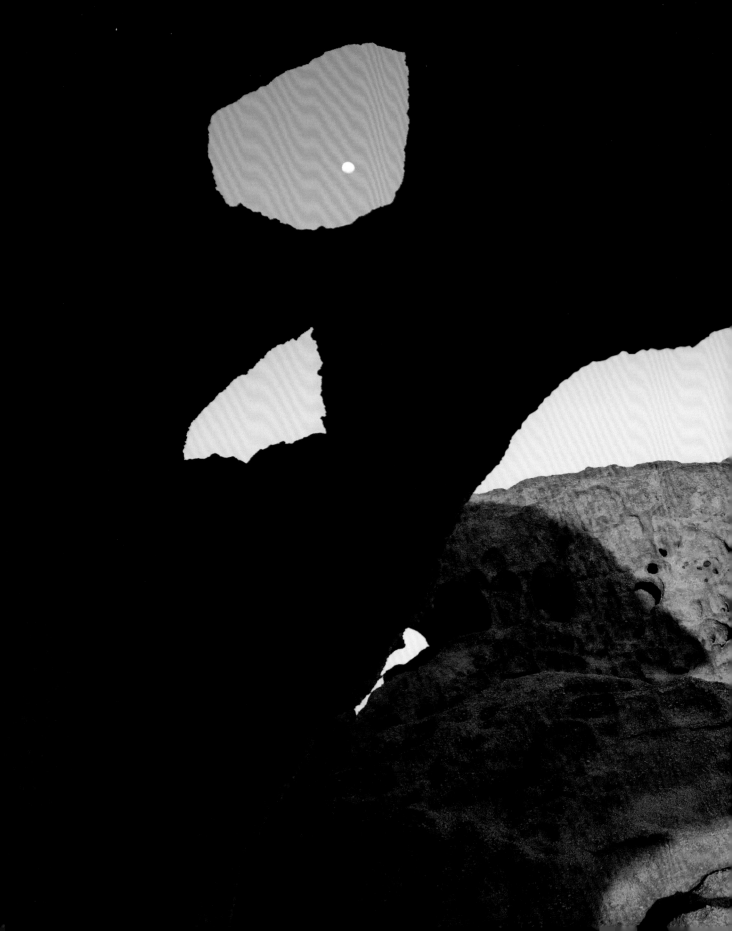

by wind and blown against the hard granite surface. The heavier, often harder grains are carried lower down by the wind, and the lighter, softer ones travel at a higher level. Over geological time, the resulting differential in granular erosion carves deeper into the lower part of the granite structure, and less so higher up. Such corrasion, coupled with the effects of extreme temperature changes over million of years, has shaped the fantastic figures at Wustenquell, inspiring names such as Elephant Rock, Eagle's Rock, the Skull and the Wave, to name a few.

Variation in the hardness of the rock, coupled with the presence of a white silica dyke, has resulted in the erosional sculpting of a seemingly perfectly sized row of teeth on this bizarre anthropomorphic profile.

Opposite
'The Wave' is one of the grandest and most spectacular tafoni forms at Wustenquell, and a perfect demonstration of differentiated granular erosion at work.

CHAPTER 10

BORNHARDTS

As you drive across the Namibian vastness on a seemingly endless road, straight as an arrow, a wake of thick dust rears up behind the vehicle and lingers in the hot air before slowly filtering back down over the flat and rugged land. For long hours of driving, this plume of dust can be the only relief – however ephemeral – across 360° of featureless landscape. Then, slowly, a real elevation point, big and solid, may rise from the flat monotony: a bornhardt looms in the distance.

The sculpting of this natural bridge, viewed from under the famous arch of the Grosse Spitzkoppe, shows the immense power of desert winds that have blown here for thousands of years. Paired with extreme thermal shocks, the scouring action of wind and wind-blown sand – called 'corrasion' – has loosened the granite particles, sculpting the rock, polishing the surface, and even perforating the granite walls and forming so-called 'corrasion hollows'.

137–124 MILLION YEARS AGO

TRAPPED BENEATH THE SURFACE

A bornhardt, or inselberg, is a geomorphological feature consisting of a prominent, isolated residual dome (or a group of domes) rising abruptly, up to a few hundred metres high, in the midst of a flat plain. The name 'bornhardt' comes from F. Wilhelm Bornhardt (1864–1946), a German explorer in Tanganyika, who first described the feature; the synonymous name 'inselberg' comes from the German and means 'island mountain'.

Major tectonic events 135 million years ago triggered the rise of rocks from deep down in the Earth's mantle towards the surface. In such events, some rocks reach the surface through dykes or fractures, and pour out in volcanic eruptions, in the form of lava – igneous rocks that have crystallized rapidly on the Earth's surface, where they are cooled by the air.

Some rocks do not reach the surface, however, but remain trapped several kilometres below the Earth's crust, where they cool and crystallize very slowly. The slow cooling process results in the growth of large crystals, as can be seen in granite. Granitic magma bodies that remain trapped underground are known as 'plutons'.

Over geological time, weathering erodes and washes away thousands of metres of rock from the surface, which is constantly lowered until the buried plutonic rock is unearthed. Because plutonic rock is harder than the neighbouring rocks, it is more erosion-resistant and remains standing proud of the surrounding, extensively eroded plains.

Their hard rock structure means that bornhardts weather in a specific manner called 'circumdenudation', which smoothes and rounds the igneous rocks, much as one peels an onion, removing one layer after another.

Bornhardts can mostly be found in hot, arid and semi-arid areas, popping up in the middle of vast, weathered landscapes. They are the visible manifestations of pluton formation that occurred during ancient geological times, and now in a

Today, the clusters of Grosse Spitzkoppe, Klein Spitzkoppe and the Pondok Mountains rise high and almost magically from the flat, eroded plain in western Namibia. These granitic magma bodies formed some 135 Ma, several kilometres below the surface.

Following pages

To the east of the Kunene region, tyre tracks carry one's gaze to the far horizon where there's a hint of relief from the endless stretches of flat desert: bornhardts rising up like islands in a sea of sand.

late stage of the erosion cycle. But the process of pluton formation never stops – new plutons are constantly being formed in volcanic areas around the globe. With time and the ongoing effects of weathering and erosion, they too will one day be exposed.

THE GROSSE AND KLEINE SPITZKOPPE BORNHARDTS

Located in central western Namibia, some 40 km northwest of Usakos and north of the road to Henties Bay, the Grosse Spitzkoppe is a huge, 30 km² inselberg, rising like a rocky island some 670 m above the sandy floor of the Namib plains. Impressive in size and shape, it stands, together with the nearby Pontok Mountains and the Klein Spitzkoppe, as a landmark of the area, as well as of Namibia itself. The Grosse Spitzkoppe, also known as the 'Matterhorn of Africa', is a declared national monument and provides a challenge to many a rock climber.

The Spitzkoppe bornhardts belong to the Damaraland Intrusive Complex in Namibia. They are part of the Paraná-Etendeka Large Igneous Province, which is one of the largest volcanic/plutonic complexes known on Earth – an intrusive complex that was formed during the Gondwana break-up, 137–124 Ma, when the South Atlantic Ocean opened up.

CHAPTER 11

BULL'S PARTY GRANITES

The extraordinary landscape on show at 'Bull's Party', found on the Ameib Farm at the foot of the Erongo Mountains, disturbs our understanding of balance and stability. The oversized boulders appear to have been scattered around by some inspired and daring gallery owner; how these massive granite formations can stand upright with such limited contact with the ground seems to defy logic. But even the most bewildering geological mysteries have an explanation.

Precariously balanced, the giant granitic boulders on the Ameib Farm northeast of Windhoek at the foot of the Erongo Mountains are some of the most geologically thought-provoking wonders of Namibia.

130–110 MILLION YEARS AGO

IDIOSYNCRATIC EROSION

The Bull's Party is located in the south of the Erongo Volcanic Complex (EVC), within the granite zone. The EVC is a well-preserved caldera structure, 30 km in diameter, surrounded by a granitic ring dyke and a mafic volcanic cone sheet. It is an erosional remnant of a bowl-shaped volcanic massif, cross-cut by resurgent plugs of granodiorite and granite bodies. This igneous complex is associated with the continental flood basalts of the Paraná-Etendeka Province – linked with the opening of the South Atlantic Ocean – and the Tristan da Cunha hotspot, located under the world's most remote inhabited island, in the South Atlantic.

During the huge Paraná-Etendeka volcanic episode, the granite structure that stayed trapped under the Earth's surface some 130–110 million years ago cooled down slowly. After a long erosion process the structure is now exposed at the surface, in the same way as Wustenquell's granite domes have been exposed. It presents some idiosyncratic erosion features, such as large domes, arches, polygonal fracture patterns, remarkable weathering pits, exfoliation and mushroom features and, most striking of all, a large number of rather precariously balanced boulders.

GRANITIC CHAOS OF BULL'S PARTY

Granites are extremely hard and resistant rock bodies when they happen to be located in temperate environments. But, despite their intrinsic resistance, they are very sensitive to erosion and wide temperature variations. This is why, in arid zones, they are easily altered by the combined action of natural agents: water (air humidity due to fog, occasional torrential rains), extreme temperature fluctuations, exposure to the sun, and corrasion by wind (see also chapter 9). When all these factors combine over millions of years, granitic chaos, as at Bull's Party, can ensue.

As water runs over the exposed granite surface, it gradually carves out trenches that widen over time. Progressively, the combined action of water and temperature changes along the cracks, dykes and fractures results in smaller blocks breaking away from the plutonic body until they are left standing as independent granite boulders,

Opposite

Erosion is the main agent at work on granites, rounding and polishing all available material, from giant rocks to tiny pebbles.

Following pages

Eroded, crumbled granite forms 'mineral sponges' that retain water. Wherever the elements deposit them, these sponges chemically dig hollows into the granitic bedrock, forming indentations called 'weathering pits'. Over time, these can come to resemble impressive granite bathtubs.

sometimes at surprising angles. The continuous erosive action of wind and rain water on their surface rounds them progressively to a spherical shape, which offers the least resistance to environmental forces.

Crumbled granite resulting from such erosion begins to form 'mineral sponges' that retain, and so prevent evaporation of, water. Either at the base of the granitic boulders, or wherever the wind or flowing water has deposited them, these granitic sponges chemically dig hollows into the granitic bedrock. They form indentations called 'weathering pits', which can, over time, become enlarged to resemble impressive granite bathtubs.

At a later stage, when the crystallized structure of the granite has broken down into coarse sand, the crumbled granite becomes a wind-driven erosive agent itself. As the abrasive particles are flung against the boulders by the wind, the heavier, often harder grains being carried lower down carve out mushroom-shaped rocks, although over time, perfect spheres are formed.

Sometimes the very base of the rock becomes so eroded that it can no longer carry the weight of the boulder. At this point, gravity takes over and the snapped-off boulder rolls down the slope, coming to rest with the chaotic pile of other escaped boulders.

As individual entities, the boulders and blocks become even more sensitive to daily thermic variations. In this area, temperatures can range from negative values during the night up to 80°C on the hottest days. When such variations occur in a short time, they can brutally weaken the crystallized structure of the granite. A sudden heavy downpour in the middle of an extremely hot day can split boulders in two, as if they had been sliced with a sword. This phenomenon is called 'core crack'.

Along with vertical erosion, the granite surface is also eroded horizontally. This phenomenon, typical of arid climates, happens when rain water cannot penetrate the rock and so remains trapped under a thin, superficial layer of the granite. When the water freezes at subzero temperatures, the newly created ice sheet expands and lifts up the thin layer of granite above it, thus creating a specific erosion pattern called 'exfoliation'. This takes place parallel to the surface of the rock, which peels off in layers, much like an onion.

Walking at the foot of the Bull's Party granites is overwhelming not only because of their scale, but also because of the astonishing opportunity it presents to examine what were magmatic and plutonic chambers in remote geological times.

CHAPTER 12

DESERTS AND HOW THEY FORMED

Deserts are among nature's most ancient and magnificent geological art works. While appearing to represent vastness and emptiness, they are, surprisingly, also home to highly developed and intriguing life forms. Namibia, the driest country in sub-Saharan Africa, encompasses some of the world's most extraordinary deserts. The Namib Desert, said to be the oldest desert on Earth, stretches for more than 2,000 km along the Atlantic coast, from the Olifants River in South Africa to the Carunjamba River in Angola; the 'fossil' Kalahari Desert lies in the eastern parts of the country; and there are other desert features in various parts of the country, such as pans and vleis.

The desert landscapes of Namibia run seamlessly into the ocean. At Spencer Bay, under the vast sweep of a soft blue sky, the vista extends, remote and dreamlike, across a region that is accessible only to a lucky few. Here, fingers of sand and sea interweave against a backdrop of imposing mountain massifs.

60 MILLION YEARS AGO TO PRESENT

CLIMATIC PHENOMENA

Deserts can be defined as climatic phenomena, for drought is the main source of all such arid regions. The absence, or near absence, of precipitation in specific zones of our planet creates a hostile environment for both fauna and flora. Water deprivation leads to exhaustion of the vegetation, gradually exposing the surface to increasing denudation. Furthermore, the huge variation in temperature between day and night smashes desert rocks into pieces, and the pieces into grains. Rare downpours generate flash floods that lead to further erosion, and carry away all detritus in their path. On the flat desert landscapes, the wind is a key player, using rock particles as yet another tool of erosion: it further alters the surface rocks and, through constant abrasion, transforms the particles into sand. Grains of sand are carried by the predominant wind and are piled up behind natural obstacles, inside depressions and, finally, spread over plains. As the sand accumulates, dunes form and multiply. Over time, this process results in seas of sand that keep moving, not unlike the waves of the ocean.

Depending on local geographic features, such as the direction and force of the wind, and on the quantity of accumulated material, sand dunes form in varied shapes, heights and colours. Linear dunes running along straight, parallel lines can be formed by the predominant wind. These dunes are longer than they are broad – as long as 400 km, and perhaps only 600 m wide – with straight or slightly curvy summits.

If mobile sand is scarce, dunes form crescent-shaped patterns, called 'barkhans' – the most common shape of dunes on Earth. They are also present on Mars, providing good proof of the presence of wind on the red planet. The dune turns its 'back' to the blast, and the outstretched 'horns' of the crescent point in the direction of the wind. These dunes can travel distances of about 100 m per year, overcoming any obstacle in their way. The most imposing barkhans on Earth have been observed in the Taklamakan Desert in China: the two 'horns' of the crescent in some cases lying over 3km apart!

Where the wind blows in equal strength from several directions, sand dunes can be star-shaped, with a central peak. They are also known as 'pyramidal dunes'.

Desertification is not only a natural phenomenon. Sadly, it is also triggered by anthropic activities such as carelessly ignited bush fires or deliberate deforestation for intensive agriculture and farming, and even for poaching. It is estimated that desertification threatens more than 20% of the Earth's land surface, arid or semi-arid zones covering 30–40 million km². Since 1980, some 200,000 km² of land is thought to have been reduced to desert each year. Regrettably, Africa is known as the 'fire continent' for the practice of land burning; by far the quickest and easiest way to clear land for agriculture, burning has been widely used for grassland management through the ages. Farmers are further encouraged by the misapprehension that this method enhances the quality of soils. On the contrary, however, land burning actually activates deforestation and ends up impoverishing the soil in the long term, ultimately sterilizing it. Land burning also generates major atmospheric pollution by carbon dioxide and airborne particles.

Cracked mud in the desolate Deadvlei clay pan is punctuated by black, roughly 900-year-old acacia skeletons. Here, in the Namib-Naukluft National Park, the sand dunes are among the highest in the world.

Right
Deforestation is, unfortunately, triggered not only by natural phenomena; as in so many other parts of Africa, land-burning is widely practised in Namibia for farming and agriculture; and, criminally, for poaching as well.

The straight road between Aus and Lüderitz that runs along the Sperrgebiet offers sweeping views of mountains, with Mount Tschaukaib peaking at 1,068 m above sea level.

Opposite

Rare, often ephemeral water sources in the Etosha National Park attract animals from near and far. Here, the natural hierarchy dictates that when an elephant herd walks briskly to the waterhole, all other animals quickly back off until the giants have quenched their thirst.

DESERTS OF NAMIBIA

The Namib Desert

Petrified sand dunes, known as 'aeolianites' and found in Tsondab's red-brown sandstone formation in the Namib Desert, indicate the existence of a proto-Namib desert in the Lower Miocene (21 Ma). Although there is still much debate about this, the age of the formation makes the Namib Desert the oldest known desert on Earth. It is also the largest desert in Namibia, stretching along the entire Atlantic coastline from the South African to the Angolan borders, in an 80–120 km-wide belt between the Atlantic Ocean and the Great Western Escarpment. Between the town of Lüderitz and the Kuiseb River lies the modern Namib Sand Sea, where the most impressive and best-known sand dunes of Namibia occur.

The immediate coastal tract is dominated by light-coloured, high, crescent dunes that form a massive sand wall against the ocean. This coastal desert is a result of the cold, upwelling Benguela Current that flows north from Antarctica along the west coast of Africa, all the way to Angola. As a consequence of the low sea temperature, little evaporation takes place – hence the extreme aridity of the adjacent Namib Desert, with 0–50 mm rainfall per year. When the cold sea air collides with the warm overland air from the Hadley Cell, an alternative source of moisture is generated: a thick fog rolls in along the coast, especially in the morning, reaching up to 50 km inland and supporting a wide variety of endemic flora and fauna. This fog, together with stormy waves and strong currents, is also responsible for sinking many ships off Namibia: more than 1,000 shipwrecks litter the appropriately named Skeleton Coast.

The harsh Kalahari Desert, where temperatures range from 70°C (on the sand) during the day to -10°C on winter nights, is home to the meerkat. These highly sociable little mammals live in organized societies of 10–30 individuals. While most of the group goes out foraging, others stay behind to babysit new cubs, and appointed sentries stand on top of mounds, watching for predators. Alarm calls quickly bring the band back to their burrows to hide.

Opposite
The Namib Desert's sea of sand offers a painterly scene that would require a palette of many colours.

Sunsets at waterholes in the Etosha National Park are a treat, when the fierce heat of the day gives way to the temperate evening, and animals make their way to the local pan for a drink.

The oryx (or gemsbok) is symbolic of Namibia, appearing on the national coat of arms. This unusual desert animal is able to limit its body temperature to below 45°C, and that of its brain to less than 42°C, thanks to a unique system of blood vessels. Oryx can survive extreme drought, quenching their thirst with dew from desert plants, or humidity from unearthed bulbs and roots.

The Namib Sand Sea is crossed by linear dunes varying from pink to vivid orange. They stretch for over 100 km and reach 120 m in height. The eastern margin is characterized by star dunes up to 220 m high – some even exceeding 300 m – and by a network of lower, partly vegetated dunes of a striking orange-red colour. Outside this sandy strip, the Namib is a rocky desert.

A treasure-trove of plants and animals lives along this lonely tract of land, many diverse species having adapted to these extreme conditions. Among the extraordinary plants are the fragile, jewel-like lichens, euphorbias, lithops or 'stone plants' and the weird *Welwitschia mirabilis* plant, which can survive without water for many seasons and lives for more than 1,000 years. Some of the remarkable animals are the sidewinding Peringuey's viper, the shovel-snouted lizard, which appears to dance on the hot sand, the Namib dune gecko, which licks its large eyeballs in order to quench its thirst, and the toktokkie or fog-basking beetle, which stands on its head on the dunes, allowing early-morning dew to condense on its body and run down towards its mouth. Despite the scarcity of food and water, big mammals have also adapted to this unforgiving environment: the oryx or gemsbok, the jackal, the brown hyaena and the endemic desert elephant (see also chapter 15) all dwell in this inhospitable land. The magnificent, desert-adapted, black-maned Kalahari lion is also found here. Thanks to its larger paws and leaner limbs than in the usual *Panthera leo*, it is able to survive in

The giant red dune of the Namib Desert – called Big Daddy – looms 325 m above the surrounding sands of Sossusvlei. An icon of Namibia, it is likely one of the tallest and most photographed dunes in the world.

the never-ending expanses of sand; but with only about 150 remaining individuals, it is now a highly endangered population.

Towards the eastern part of the Namib Desert, multidirectional winds have formed a cluster of star dunes that make up one of the most famous landscapes of Namibia: Sossusvlei. Enriched with iron oxide, this red sand has been accumulating in the area for the last 5 Ma, covering the pre-existing desert (aged 30 Ma) that lies over the rock complex of Rehoboth (aged 1 Ga). Sandstones belonging to the Rehoboth Complex can be seen today as they emerge in the form of inselbergs amid the flat surrounding lands. Sossusvlei is situated on the interior delta of the ephemeral Tsauchab River. This is where in years of exceptional rainfall – which may happen only a few times every century – the river reaches Sossusvlei and, after flowing through the dunes, disappears into the sand. By so doing, the river leaves behind layers of grey clay sediments as well as saltpans amid the red sand dunes. Over time, some pans have become so isolated by the dunes that no further water can reach them, neither from the river, nor from the drying aquifer. A resulting phenomenon is the white clay pan of Deadvlei. Originally bathed in water from the flooding Tsauchab River, the area was populated by camel thorn trees. As the erratic movement of the dunes diverted the ephemeral river in other directions, the Deadvlei area became totally deprived of water some 900 years ago. The trees quickly died and dried under the scorching sun, but have not decomposed as a result of the dryness of the climate. Their black skeletons have remained standing ever since.

Across the endless, desolate vastness of the Namib Desert between Lüderitz and Walvis
Bay, erosion has removed kilometres of rock, leaving what looks almost like the skeleton
of the Earth, made of metamorphic rocks crisscrossed by dyke injections.

The ochre Kalahari sand dunes show their wild side – two young lion brothers on the lookout.

Opposite

The coastal winds of the Atlantic Ocean carve some of the tallest sand dunes in the world – some reaching 300 m in height – in the vast Namib Desert. The dunes are sometimes invaded by fast-flowing rivers during rainy periods, as in this aerial view of the Namib-Naukluft National Park.

The Kalahari Desert

In the eastern part of the country the Kalahari Desert has formed mainly over the last 186,000 years. The desert, of which 930,000 km^2 lies in Botswana, Namibia and South Africa, extends into seven different countries. Unlike the Namib Desert, the Kalahari Desert does not feature impressive dunes; rather, it is characterized by undulating plains where low-range dunes form successive waves. The Kalahari dunes are known for the deep ochre hue of their sand, which appears to be ablaze at sunrise and sunset.

Satellite image was acquired by Landsat 7's Enhanced Thematic Mapper plus (ETM+) sensor on August 12, 2000.

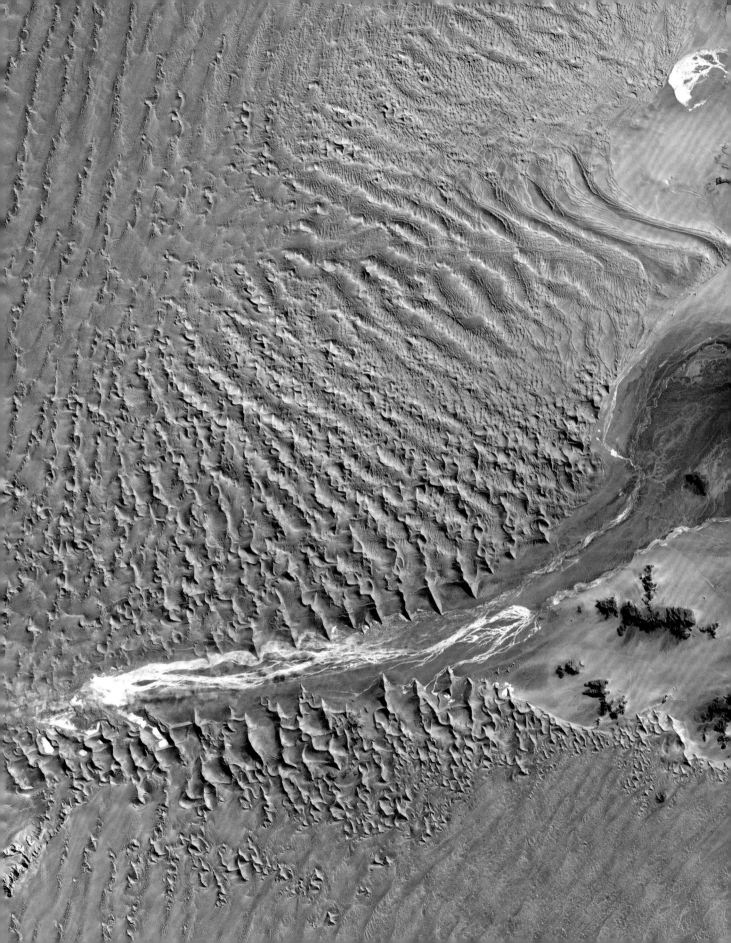

In spite of being labelled a desert, the Namibian sector of the Kalahari Desert receives a fair amount of annual rainfall, and has enough ephemeral rivers and aquifers to sustain both a prolific flora and varied wildlife, including mammals, birds and insects, which have all adapted to the relatively arid conditions. Not least of these is the iconic black-maned Kalahari lion, which roams the ochre crests of the dunes.

Etosha Pan

The 4,760 km^2 Etosha Pan, a large inland basin situated in northern Namibia, is one of the iconic features of the country, with its enduringly barren scenery. It lies within the Etosha National Park – one of the largest wildlife national parks in the country.

It took tens of millions of years for the Damara Belt to disintegrate, the erosion debris accumulating at its base, thus forming a vast alluvial plain in the southernmost part of the Owambo Basin. At a time of very heavy rainfall, a lake developed inside this depression, fed by rivers from the north and east, such as the Kunene River, which at that time would have followed a different route. As the climate became more arid, the lake progressively dried up, depositing huge quantities of minerals such as salt, gypcrete and calcrete, which is an accumulation of predominantly calcium carbonate, and can be 30–120 m thick in the Etosha Pan. Nevertheless, Damara-sourced groundwater continued to feed the depression, forming artesian springs. The combined action of groundwater and of ephemeral rivers has progressively increased the mineral deposits, leading to the formation of a flat saltpan, baked by the scorching southern African sun and swept by eroding winds.

Today, three climatic periods prevail at the Etosha National Park: January to April is hot and wet, with approximately 430 mm of precipitation – although evaporation is estimated to exceed rainfall; May to August is cold and dry; and the remainder of the year is hot and dry.

Thanks to the presence of surface- and groundwater, as well as water from drilled boreholes, the Etosha National Park – and its apparently barren and inhospitable pan, shimmering with heat – is home to 114 mammal species, 340 bird species (a third of which are migratory) and a variety of trees.

Opposite

When the large Etosha Pan is at its driest, colours become muted under the scorching sun. Oryx and springbok cross the vast surface in search of waterholes, feeding on whatever vegetation they can find.

Following pages

The haunting beauty of Sossusvlei confronts us with elements both mortal and immortal. On the one hand, the ever-blowing wind continuously churns and tosses the restless sea of sand. On the other, the life of once-living trees has been snuffed out, leaving just their 'fossilized' remains standing as though part of some vast modern art installation.

CHAPTER 13

NATURAL ARENA FOR ART

The wealth of parietal art around the world – the archaeological term for artwork applied on natural walls or large blocks of stone – provides striking material evidence of early humans' search for meaning. It suggests that people, as they have evolved, have sought to give meaning to their presence, to communicate with their fellow beings and express their sense of spirituality by means of inscriptions and paintings.

Studies of these early works suggest that they were linked to intense ritual activities, possibly relating to fertility and successful hunting.

Twyfelfontein has the largest known collection of rock engravings and paintings on the African continent. While Twyfelfontein may be a relatively new name, this old freshwater spring was already known by people in prehistoric times. And 200–170 million years ago – long before humans strolled across this land – the Etjo sandstone that would become their 'canvas' was progressively deposited by the ever-present winds.

35,000 YEARS AGO

A panel of Etjo sandstone provided an opportunity for this scene of an otherworldly lion with five toes on each paw, thought to be a shaman who transformed into a lion during a trance. Reinhard Maack, who discovered the Brandberg's White Lady site in 1918, reported on the astounding series of rock engravings at Twyfelfontein in the Kunene Region of northwestern Namibia.

TRACING HUMAN HISTORY

Since the birth of archaeology during the Renaissance period, archaeologists have studied such traces, dating as far back as palaeo-human societies and leaving a valuable record of life through the ages. Not only can scientists decipher historical information about ancient people's daily life – their tools, habitats, feeding methods; but they can also deduce something of their intangible culture – their dreams, hopes, fears and torments, and even their connection with the afterlife, revealed through shamanism and initiation rites. Archaeologists term this information the 'intangible heritage' of civilizations.

Parietal art – in Namibia as much as elsewhere – is as inextricably intertwined with geological features as are natural elements such as the Brandberg and Spitzkoppe. Because much of the 'wall art' would have required some preparation and even painstaking labour, we know that the places where early humans have left signs on walls or rocks were places where they could stay: water would have been available nearby, and caves would have offered reliable shelter from predators and harsh weather conditions. In such safe environments, pundits, priests, scribes and artists could let their imagination and talent run freely on the walls; they could comment on daily life as well as interpret the 'greater life', expressing their dreams and beliefs about the supernatural world.

Initially applying paint to the walls with their fingers, artists would quickly have turned to locally available materials: flintstone for etching, seashells as paint containers, pads of moss as sponges, animal hair or vegetable fibre for brushes, charcoal for drawing, hollowed bones for spraying paint. Colour pigments were also sourced locally, mostly from minerals found in the earth: ochre clay for brown, yellow and red, and manganese dioxide or charcoal for black. By grinding the pigments and mixing them with cave water rich in calcium carbonate, and adding animal blood and fat, human urine, crushed bones and vegetable extracts, artists ensured that the colours would stick and harden firmly onto the rock surface.

Although Namibia's intangible heritage is rather poorly documented at this stage, scientific investigation into parietal art will almost certainly reveal new insights into the country's social history.

THE WHITE LADY OF THE BRANDBERG

An extensive hike along the usually dry Tsisab River bed, across the protected area of the Brandberg range, is required to reach the site of the 'White Lady' – and visitors are assigned a local guide to guard against anyone tampering with the paintings. There, sheltered by a rock ledge, a masterpiece of rock painting has been standing for 16,000 years, despite the ill-treatment meted out by tourists of a bygone age, who used to throw water at the painting to enhance its hues – and fatally damaged the sharpness of the contours and colours. This most famous of Namibia's rock paintings was discovered in 1918 by German explorer Reinhard Maack, and is just one of tens

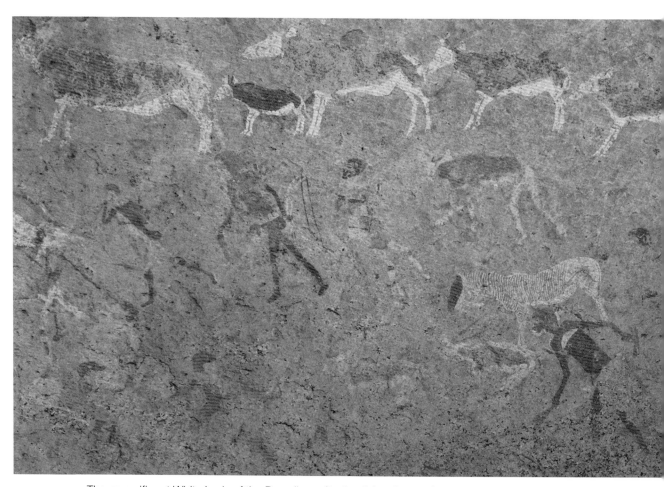

The magnificent White Lady of the Brandberg (to the right of centre), surrounded by cattle and hunters, reveals the talent of early hunter-gatherer artists of the region. The Brandberg range lies near the coast in the northwestern Namib Desert.

of thousands of rock paintings scattered across the Brandberg range. Mesmerized by this painting in particular, Maack described the central figure as a warrior depicted in a style showing Egyptian and Mediterranean influences.

After reading Maack's discovery report and assessing the striking similarities of the White Lady to drawings of athletes discovered on the Greek island of Knossos, French Catholic priest and anthropologist Abbé Breuil set up his own expedition into the Brandberg. He was to become haunted by the mysterious beauty of the White Lady, 'a very young woman, with a singularly exquisite profile, reminiscent of a figure on an ancient Greek vase'. On his return home he published his theory on the Mediterranean origin of this rock painting, which proposed the early presence of Greeks in this part of Africa – a notion that was viewed with scepticism.

This inspired but fanciful interpretation was finally rejected by historian Basil Davidson in 1963, when he convincingly established that this rock painting, along with thousands of other paintings on the Brandberg and across Damaraland, was simply the work of local hunter-gatherer San.

Small groups of hunters evidently lived in the upper parts of the mountain during the dry season, when little water and food could be obtained in the surrounding dry plains. The mountain, with its well-formed sheet-joint structure, provided abundant small aquifers that sustained life in the dry times. Interestingly, the rock painting sites are all to be found in the vicinity of these reliable fountains.

Following pages

These cross-legged men have been named the 'two tailors'; but one of them could just as well be a yogi sitting on a rock, teaching his followers.

TWYFELFONTEIN'S ROCK ENGRAVINGS

Twyfelfontein (the 'uncertain spring' in Afrikaans) lies in a remote semi-arid area in Damaraland in northern central Namibia, at the head of a valley running north–south and carrying a small tributary of the Huab River. The valley is bounded by sandstones of the Etjo Formation and shales of the Gai-As Formation, which are underlain by dark Kuiseb Formation schists of the Damara Sequence. Freshwater springs appear at the contact zone of impermeable clay layers and porous sandstones and sand formations. Such is the case at the Twyfelfontein spring, which comes to life only when the porous sandstone has absorbed enough water following good rains. The presence of this small spring has attracted people and game for a long time, especially hunting communities, where the hunters could observe passing game, unseen, from a rocky terrace some 50 m above the spring.

The sandstone of the Etjo Formation weathers in two different ways, depending on its hardness. The softer rock weathers into tafoni (see chapter 9), which creates reliable shelters; the harder rocks are transformed into large, flat-faced blocks that provide a suitable surface for rock carving.

Desert varnish is a striking and rare geomorphic phenomenon, the result of many processes taking place over geological time. It forms only on the exposed surface of pavements in desert landforms, and is well represented at Twyfelfontein. The varnish source materials are primarily airborne dust which, together with direct aqueous atmospheric depositions, forms an extremely thin coating of a dark, orange-yellow to black substance composed of about 30% iron and manganese oxides, and up to 70% clay minerals. It was clearly the preferred base for rock carving and engraving as it enables the artist to play with a variety of naturally available colours.

It is on these natural canvases that almost 2,000 images have been recorded, all within a limited area (less than 1 km^2) around Twyfelfontein. This open-air gallery contains the largest prehistoric rock-engraving site in Namibia – and one of the largest in Africa. In 1952 it was proclaimed a national monument of Namibia, and it was listed as a World Heritage Site in 2007. The rock engravings include an extraordinary diversity of wild animals: more than 200 giraffes, 100 rhinos, as well as elephants, oryx, ostriches, impalas, zebras, a lion, a dancing kudu, and many more. The engravings are thought to have been created by San hunter-gatherers over a period spanning about 2,000 years, starting some 6,000 years ago. It is believed that the images found at Twyfelfontein are (like much of the parietal art of Africa) not so much a naturalistic representation of daily life, but rather of a highly symbolic nature and most probably related to shamanism.

Circles, dots, grids and spirals representing the wholeness of the universe surround the figure of the 'dancing kudu', possibly the most famous engraving at Twyfelfontein. This supernatural pregnant human-kudu is thought to be the incarnation of a shaman in a trance for accessing special powers to help his fellow humans.

CHAPTER 14

A WEALTH OF GEMS AND MINERALS

Mineral deposits arise from three major processes: magmatic, metamorphic and sedimentary, and Namibia shows evidence of all three. Mineral bodies do not form just anywhere: their formation requires specific conditions relating to pressure and temperature, triggered by the composition of the local geological environment, as well as the circulation of fluids taking place during magmatic or metamorphic events.

The remains of a diamond-mining station amid the desolate dunes of the Namib Desert, at its most remote here, midway between the towns of Lüderitz and Walvis Bay.

20TH CENTURY

GEODES AND KARSTIC GALLERIES

In the case of magmatic and metamorphic origins, such as in the Damara Orogeny (resulting from subduction or collision of tectonic plates), hot material intruded through the host rock triggers a chemical reaction on its way up to the surface. In addition to the minerals already present in the magma, the high-pressured and super-heated fluids that go with it leach, dissolve and incorporate minerals present inside the host rock as they advance upwards. Precipitation of minerals occurs inside local 'mineral traps' such as shear zones, fractures and pockets. This process is what forms mineral veins and the peculiar geological bodies known as 'geodes'.

Minerals can also develop from weathered sedimentary rock formations. In such cases, host rocks are eroded over time by rains, and minerals dissolved in the rain water are slowly deposited into topographic 'traps'. This is how the world-famous Tsumeb Mine was formed: quantities of minerals were deposited inside a 1,000 m-long, nearly vertical karstic gallery, where 247 different mineral species were later identified – 52 of them for the very first time anywhere.

THE RAREST OF THEM ALL

The same process applies to Namibian diamonds. Diamond, like common graphite, is a form of pure carbon (C), one of the most common elements in the universe. But diamond is also the hardest, the rarest and the most fascinating of all natural substances, which is why it is so valuable. Very high temperatures and pressures are required for the formation of natural diamonds – conditions that occur in limited zones of the Earth's mantle, about 150 km below the surface, where temperatures are at least 1,050°C. These conditions are not present globally; instead, they are thought to occur primarily in the mantle beneath the stable interiors of continental plates, or cratons.

Diamonds formed and stored in these 'diamond stability zones' are delivered to the Earth's surface during deep-source volcanic eruptions, where pieces of the mantle are torn away and carried rapidly to the surface. These eruptions produce the kimberlite and lamproite pipes that are sought after by diamond prospectors. Kimberlite pipes are found only in Archaean-aged cratons – areas of rock that are at least 2.5 Ga. The first kimberlite pipe was discovered on the Kaapvaal Craton near the town of Kimberley, South Africa, hence its name. Numerous kimberlite pipes have since been found on the Kaapvaal Craton, which extends through parts of South Africa, Botswana and Zimbabwe.

A rusty old sign hangs on a hotel wall, the relic of a bygone time when diamonds, brought to the surface by ancient volcanic eruptions, were to be found along the Namibian coastal regions. Diamond mining is still alive and kicking today, although it has moved offshore of the Sperrgebiet (forbidden area), and is now mainly conducted in the deep waters of the Atlantic Ocean.

Weathering causes the kimberlite to release its diamonds from their magmatic envelope. These gems are then carried away by rain and rivers and deposited into topographic traps such as river beds or sedimentary zones of streams and coastlines. Research has shown that, over the past 90 million years, most of the drainage basins covering the Kaapvaal Craton have flowed from east to west and emptied into the Atlantic Ocean. Initially, the diamonds would have been concentrated in small tidal channels of river deltas and on nearby beaches. They would later be widely redistributed along Namibia's coastline.

In fact, although kimberlite and lamproite volcanic pipe structures are present in Namibia, they do not contain diamonds. Instead, Namibia's diamonds come from pipes in Botswana and South Africa, and have been carried over into Namibia by rivers. Because of their long journey, the diamonds have become widely dispersed across both terrestrial and marine locations.

Namibia's southwestern coast, the Sperrgebiet, hosts one of the world's largest gem diamond deposits. Well over 100 million carats of gem-quality diamonds have been extracted here since the initial discovery of diamonds in the area in 1908. Namibia is one of the world's major producers of diamonds, 95% of which are of gem quality. It is the sixth largest diamond producer in Africa (2.5% of total output) and diamond mining alone accounts for 5.8% of its GDP.

THE GHOST TOWN OF KOLMANSKOP

Sometimes, diamonds are found lying on the Earth's surface. This is how they were discovered at Kolmanskop, 15 km inland from the windswept port of Lüderitz on the Atlantic coast, amid the engulfing Namib Desert dunes.

In April 1908, a specimen of this special crystalline form of carbon was discovered by worker Zecharias Lewala as he was shovelling drift sand off the railway line at Kolmanskop. Workers had been asked by August Stauch – a recently arrived German romantic convinced that sand in this part of the world held natural treasures – to look out for diamonds. Lewala picked up a glittering stone and handed it to Stauch, who headed immediately for Swakopmund where he could have the shiny stone analysed at a minerals laboratory. A visiting European gem expert confirmed that the stone was a diamond. Back in Lüderitz, Stauch founded the Colonial Mining Company to explore the ground for which he had submitted a hasty claim. As the story went out

Kolmanskop offers evidence that diamonds are not necessarily for ever! What became in its heyday the boom town of Namibia, when 5 million carats of diamonds were extracted between 1908 and 1914, suddenly died when World War I and new discoveries elsewhere brought an abrupt end to the town's flourishing activity. Kolmanskop's sand-filled homes symbolize the impermanence of humans, their structures and their dreams.

that diamonds could be harvested by the scoop, a diamond rush ensued, similar to the California Gold Rush of the mid-19th century. By now a boom town, Kolmanskop welcomed the newly installed mine management and workers' families, together with the usual crowd of fortune hunters coming from far and wide. Not only were the stones of the utmost quality – the grade higher here than any other deposit before or since – but they were extremely easy to recover. In just a few years, Kolmanskop became one of the wealthiest towns in the world; its hospital had the first X-ray unit in the southern hemisphere!

Between 1908 and 1914, some 5 million carats were extracted from the area, amounting to roughly 1,000 kg. But World War I and new mineral discoveries further south put a sudden end to the wealth of Kolmanskop. Today it's an eerie ghost town, swept by the desert sand and strong winds. Some houses are still standing, the skeleton of an electric pole, a beautifully decorated entrance door, a ballroom and a gym ... in spite of the silence, if one listens carefully, one can still hear the lively buzz of bygone days.

On 22 September 1908, barely six months after the discovery of diamonds at Kolmanskop, the Sperrgebiet (prohibited territory), which covers a 100 km-wide coastal strip between the Orange River and latitude 26° south, was proclaimed; and sole mining rights were awarded to the Deutsche Kolonial-Gesellschaft für Südwestafrika, which proceeded to exploit the diamond fields through its daughter company Deutsche Diamanten-Gesellschaft. In the five years from 1908 to 1913, 4.7 million carats of diamonds, worth about 150 million Reichsmark, were mined. After World War I, in 1920, nine companies that were engaged in diamond production in the Sperrgebiet amalgamated to form Consolidated Diamond Mines (CDM), a subsidiary of De Beers of Kimberley, who continued from then up to 1994 to hold the exclusive exploration and mining rights in the area. In 1994 the Namibian government joined this venture to form a new company, NAMDEB. At the beginning of the new century the Sperrgebiet was opened up for exploration for commodities other than precious stones, and a land-use plan was formulated to balance economic interests against environmental concerns, aimed at protecting and preserving a unique landscape. The Sperrgebiet National Park was proclaimed in 2008, and today conservation, tourism and mineral exploration co-exist, while diamond mining takes place increasingly offshore.

As a fair proportion of the world's gem-quality diamonds originate from this area, the coastal strip between Oranjemund and Lüderitz fully deserves the name of Diamond Coast. What began in 1908 with the discovery of a glittering stone by a railway worker at Kolmanskop has since developed into one of the most remarkable mining operations in history. Today, industrial mining run by De Beers continues on the seabed with highly specialized vessels mining diamonds in water depths ranging between 90 and 140 m. Harvesting of the 'most valuable of gems, known only to kings', as Roman author Pliny the Elder wrote in the first century AD, is not over.

The ocean between Oranjemund and Lüderitz is the new field of exploration for diamonds, perpetuating the glitter – and wealth – of this unique region.

Following pages

Here, the Namib Desert's drifting waves of sand meet the breaking waves of the Atlantic Ocean. This spectacular meeting of two different 'seas' defines most of the lengthy coast of Namibia, which formed as the South Atlantic Ocean progressively opened up.

TSUMEB MINE

The town of Tsumeb – from the San word *tsombtsou*, meaning 'to dig a hole that collapsed again' – was founded in 1905 for industrial mining of rare and unusual minerals in this part of the central plateau of Namibia. But the region's extraordinary richness in mineral wealth, if not its diversity, was already known to the San, as traces of copper smelting dating from early times have been discovered near what was once called the Green Hill – a large natural hill of green, oxidized copper ore that has subsequently been mined out. It did not take long for the first European explorers to find out about the hill and recognize its value. 'In the whole of my experience, I have never seen such a sight as was presented before my view at Tsumeb, and I very much doubt that I shall ever see another one like this in any other locality,' wrote Matthew Rogers on 12 January 1893 after seeing the Green Hill for the first time.

In 1893, Europeans first exploited what was to become The Tsumeb Mine, extracting more than 25 million tons of mineral ore between 1905 and 1990: antimony, silver, arsenic, cadmium, cobalt, copper, tin, gallium, germanium, mercury, nickel, lead, zinc – all of spectacular grade. The mining operation closed in 1996 for economic reasons, but Tsumeb remains a mecca among geologists, mineralogists and collectors from all over the world.

CHAPTER 15

FLOWING GROUNDWATER

Namibia generally appears to be bone dry for most of the year. Surface water appears only after heavy rainfall, when it gushes down ephemeral rivers and fills up parched saltpans. But surface water is a phenomenon that usually lasts for only a few days, if not merely hours. Most of this water never reaches the sea, but is swallowed by the thirsty ground. This does not mean it disappears, though; rather, it seeps underground, recharging aquifers that lie below the surface of river beds.

There is a breathtakingly beautiful area in the northwest of Namibia, in the midst of a huge sandy desert with desolate gravel plains, where the presence of groundwater supports wildlife – a seemingly miraculous occurrence.

True nomads of the desert, giraffes are perfectly adapted to survive in the harsh conditions characterized by scarce food, intense heat and little or no water. Along the Huab, Hoanib and Hoarusib rivers, in order to quench their thirst, they take advantage of the providential waterholes dug by desert elephants.

TODAY

A HIDDEN RESOURCE

The arid and remote area of Damaraland is edged by the Skeleton Coast and transected by the dry river beds of the Huab, the Hoanib and, further north, the Hoarusib. It is a breathtakingly beautiful area in the northwest of Namibia, although it attracts few visitors. Here, almost miraculously, in the midst of a huge sandy desert with desolate gravel plains, lives a variety of wildlife, supported by invisible groundwater. Indeed, some animals, like desert elephants, have developed the ability to access water buried below the dry surface of river beds.

Lying on the old Gondwana landmass, the area is crisscrossed by major faults. This network of faults and fractures makes an ideal system of channels for water to run from the remote highlands down towards the sea, thus creating ephemeral rivers in rare seasons of heavy rainfall. Over geological time, the force of water has not only broadened the fractures themselves but has also filled them with debris – blocks of rock, clay, sand, gravel and other material carried from upstream. These deposited

mineral elements form rocky storage structures, or aquifers. With heavy rain, the rivers flood briefly, but the running water is rapidly absorbed by the extremely porous, thirsty river bed. It infiltrates the sandy, gravelly alluvial deposits, penetrating the network of fractures and fissures, and feeding the groundwater reserves. The greater the intensity, volume and duration of the flood, the more the aquifers are recharged.

This groundwater flows on, only now it flows directly under the dry river bed. And, unlike Damaraland's surface-water rivers, which do not reach the sea, this underground flow eventually reaches the coast.

Below and following pages

It is hard to imagine that, in these desert landscapes along the western edge of the Hoanib River, water flows under the dried-out land surface, eventually reaching the ocean along the northern Skeleton Coast. This groundwater supports desert elephants and a range of other wildlife, a fact that's not immediately apparent in the barren landscape.

DESERT ELEPHANTS, THE ULTIMATE SURVIVORS

Living in this harsh and desolate environment, desert elephants have developed an amazing ability to 'smell' groundwater – up to a metre deep – and access it as needed.

Desert elephants have been found in only two locations: in Namibia and perhaps in Mali, although it's possible this latter tribe has in recent years been hunted to extinction. These elephants are not a differentiated species or subspecies, but they are unique in that they have adapted to their arid living environment by developing some specific morphological features. In particular, they have less body mass, and so require less food; and they have slightly broader feet for crisscrossing the Skeleton Coast sand dunes and rocky terrain, as well as for walking up sandy hills to cool off in the breeze at the summit during the scorching hours of heat. But the desert elephants' most extraordinary adaptation is their ability to sniff out water underground; and then, using their feet, tusks and trunk, to dig down into sandy river beds to reach the life-giving liquid. This adaptation makes them the ultimate desert survivors.

It is an enthralling sight to watch a mother digging a well in the dry Hoanib River bed, her calf by her side learning a skill that has been passed on from many generations of forebears. After digging, the elephant pauses, patiently waiting for the well to fill with water before she and her calf can quench their thirst. That done, they can then resume their slow and majestic journey along the dry river banks.

An interesting side effect of elephant-dug wells in these dry river beds is that they also benefit other local wildlife. The giraffe, jackal, oryx and springbok, as well as birds and insects, make good use of these handy waterholes to quench their thirst.

The desert-dwelling elephants that roam the barren northwest region of Namibia are limited in number. In the Hoarusib, Hoanib, and Uniab river surroundings, their total population is thought to consist of approximately 80 individuals only, living in smaller-than-average family groups of only two or three individuals. Because of their scarcity and their unique lifestyle, they are viewed as national treasures of Namibia. They have been designated top priority for protection by the International Union for the Conservation of Nature. Despite this, their population numbers dropped by approximately 30% between 2005 and 2015. And, very sadly, such a fragile survival situation did not prevent the official issuing of nine hunting permits during the summer of 2014.

Desert elephants are well adapted to surviving water and food shortages in these arid conditions. They have been known to travel up to 200 km in search of water, drinking only every three to four days, in stark contrast to a savanna elephant's daily intake of about 150 litres. The Namib's desert-adapted elephants have developed slightly longer trunks that enable them to dig deep into the sand in search of underground water. Unlike other elephants, they take great care not to destroy or pull up the trees and bushes they feed on, so as not to destroy a limited resource.

In the intense heat, evaporation – either of groundwater sucked up to the surface by the heat, or of surface flowing water – leaves a cracked residual crust of salt and minerals, known as 'calcrete'.

BIBLIOGRAPHY

Forssman, T. & Gutteridge, L. 2012. *Bushman rock art*. 30 Degrees South Publishers, Oxford. 237 pp.

Goudie, A. & Viles, H. 2015. *Landscapes and landform of Namibia*. Springer Publishers, Berlin. 173 pp.

Grünert, N. 2015. *Namibia: Geologisches Wunderland*. Padlangs Publications. 219 pp.

Grünert, N. 2013. *Namibia – Fascination of Geology – A travel handbook*. Klaus Hess Publishers, Windhoek. 255 pp.

Jouve, L. & Jouve, M. 2009. *Secret Namibia*. Struik Travel & Heritage, Cape Town. 152 pp.

Pager, S-A. 1985. *A walk through prehistoric Twyfelfontein*. Kuiseb Verlag. 24 pp.

Pager, S-A. 2008. *A visit to the white lady of the Brandberg*. Kuiseb Verlag. 23 pp.

Levinson, O. 2009. *Diamonds in the desert*. Kuiseb Verlag. 216 pp.

McCarthy, T. & Rubidge, B. 2005. *The story of Earth & Life – A southern African perspective on a 4.6-billion-year journey*. Struik Nature, Cape Town. 335 pp.

McKenzie, R. 2014. Meteorites *– A southern Africa perspective*. Struik Nature, Cape Town. 120 pp.

Mendelsohn, J., Jarvis, A., Roberts, C. & Robertson, T. 2010. *Atlas of Namibia – a portrait of the land and its people*. Sunbird Publishers, Cape Town. 200 pp.

Miller, R.McG. 2008. *The Geology of Namibia*. 3 volumes. Ministry of Mines and Energy, Geological Survey of Namibia.

Norman, N. 2010. *The extraordinary world of Diamonds*. Jacana Media, Johannesburg. 302 pp.

Schneider, G.I.C. & Schneider, M.B. 2008. *Gondwanaland Geopark – A proposed Geopark for Namibia*, 91 pp.

Schneider, G. 2008. *The roadside Geology of Namibia*. 2nd Ed. Gebrüder Borntraeger, Stuttgart. 294 pp.

Seely, M. 2010. *The Namib – Natural history of an ancient desert*. Published by the Desert Research Foundation of Namibia. 112 pp.

Wirth, V. 2010. *Lichens of the Namib Desert*. Klaus Hess Publishers, Windhoek. 96 pp.

PICTURE CREDITS

Anne-Marie Detay: Cover, half-title page, pp. 9, 10, 12-13, 15, 16-17, 18, 21, 25, 26, 32, 41, 42, 45, 46-47, 60, 70-71, 72, 74, 76, 79, 80, 84-85, 87 top, 87 bottom, 88-89, 90, 91, 92, 94, 95, 96, 98, 99, 102, 106-107, 108-109, 113, 121 left, 121 right, 122 bottom, 124, 125, 126, 127, 129, 130, 133, 136, 138, 146, 148, 150, 153, 154-155, 156, 160-161, 162, 164, back cover; Michel Detay: Title page, pp. 7, 22-23, 30, 33, 34, 36-37, 38-39, 48-49, 50-51, 57, 58, 63, 64, 65, 66, 69, 83, 100-101, 103, 104, 110, 114-115, 117, 118, 122 top, 128, 134-135, 140-141, 142-143, 145, 157-158; Others: Christian Koeberl, University of Vienna, Austria: p. 29; Johnny Bouffarigue: pp. 52, 54; Landsat 7- NASA: p.131

INDEX

Page numbers referring to pictures are given in **bold** type